HERITAGE HOUSES

OF NOVA SCOTIA

All photography by Gary Castle, with the following exceptions:
page 51-52, photos of Sherbrooke Village by Robert Jordan-Robichaud, copyright Nova Scotia Museum; page 59, photography Ann Clow, Yarmouth

Formac Publishing Company Limited acknowledges the support of the Cultural Affairs Section, Nova Scotia Department of Tourism and Culture. We acknowledge the financial support of the Government of Canada through the Book Publishing Industry Development Program (BPIDP) for our publishing activities. We acknowledge the support of the Canada Council for the Arts for our publishing program.

National Library of Canada Cataloguing in Publication Data

Archibald, Stephen
    Heritage houses of Nova Scotia / by Stephen Archibald and Sheila Stevenson.

Includes index.
ISBN 0-88780-601-5

    1. Historic buildings—Nova Scotia. 2. Architecture, Domestic—Nova Scotia—History. 3. Dwellings—Nova Scotia—History. I. Stevenson, Sheila II. Title.

NA7242.N68A72 2003   728'.09716   C2003-903785-1

Formac Publishing Company Limited
5502 Atlantic Street
Halifax NS B3H 1G4
www.formac.ca

Printed in the People's Republic of China

HERITAGE HOUSES
OF NOVA SCOTIA

Stephen Archibald and Sheila Stevenson

Photography by Gary Castle

Formac Publishing Company Limited
Halifax

Acknowledgements

When we first became interested in the housing history and cultural landscape of Nova Scotia several decades ago, there were only a few local books to provide guidance and inspiration. The Heritage Trust of Nova Scotia had begun its advocacy for preservation and recognition of the province's older buildings and districts, the Nova Scotia Museum was acquiring a collection of historic buildings, and a few individuals with a new regard for old houses were renovating them.

Now the resources are much richer. Through our work at the Nova Scotia Museum and by personally living in and renovating several nineteenth-century houses, we've been fortunate to know many people who share our interest and who have enlarged our knowledge and pleasure. When preparing this book, we were able to draw on these experiences and on the work of many colleagues and friends, who have shared the joy of examining old houses and studying the historical context in which they were built.

Although we have drawn on many sources, including local histories, we want to acknowledge in particular the following writers and photographers: Mary Byers and Margaret McBurney, Alvin Comiter, Brenda Dunn, Peter Ennals and Deryck Holdsworth, Alan Gowans, Terry James and Bill Plaskett, Harold Kalman, Joann Latremouille and Kathleen Flanagan, Mary K. MacLeod and James O. St. Clair, Virginia and Lee McAlester, Elizabeth Pacey, Allen Penney, Roy Rhyno, Barbara R. Robertson, Jean Weir, and the authors of the architectural series in the *Canadian Historic Sites: Occasional Papers in Archaeology and History*, published by the National Historic Parks and Sites Branch of Parks Canada: Mathilde Brosseau, Christina Cameron, Nathalie Clerk, Leslie Maitland, and Janet Wright. We also want to acknowledge the individuals, municipalities and organizations who have provided valuable information on their websites and the owners of private residences who agreed to have their house photographed.

This book is dedicated to the people who accept the challenge of keeping heritage houses in Nova Scotia alive and well. They keep us in touch with our history and provide us with a wonderful gift.

— Stephen Archibald and Sheila Stevenson

Contents

Acknowledgements 5

The Evolution of Nova Scotia House Styles 8

Georgian Classical 16

In the Vernacular Tradition 24

The Scottish House 38

Greek Revival 42

Gothic Revival 50

Italianate 58

Second Empire Style 66

The Halifax House 72

Lunenburg Bump Houses 80

Queen Anne 86

Stick, Shingle, Eclectic and Richardson-Romanesque 98

Craftsman and Revival Styles 108

Further Reading 127

Index 128

The Evolution of Nova Scotia House Styles

This book is about the satisfaction of getting to know Nova Scotia's houses. Heritage houses are one of Nova Scotia's most distinctive assets. They're part of the Nova Scotian landscape — in villages and towns, on secondary roads and in cities. Seeking out Nova Scotia's housing legacy can be a lot of fun and is a great reason to travel the province.

Houses embody the stories of the province's settlement history: how people and skills, traditions and ideas from various places arrived over time to create a distinctive cultural landscape. Houses, more than any other thing in our material culture, record the range of Nova Scotians' experiences and lifestyles. Exposed as they are in the landscape and streetscape, houses are our most visible and accessible legacy.

The key to knowing Nova

Scotian houses is learning their distinctive features. In this book we outline the province's housing heritage according to the various types and styles of houses that most often occur in the landscape. What do the variations in appearance tell us? Deciphering and describing the details is part of the satisfaction of house-watching. The size, the shape, the roof line, the type and location of windows, the details of entrances are all clues to the age and physical history of a house. As you drive along a country road or a town street, note what you see: a hipped roof; a pointed gable; pilasters. Once you know the style of a house, you can usually tell when it was built within a couple of decades. Generally speaking, Nova Scotians waited a few years before jumping into a new style that had already been embraced elsewhere. The range of house styles in a particular community indicate when it was prosperous, and over what period of time. Variations in style reflect the local climate as well: the pitch of the roofs on some houses in the snowier northern region of Colchester and Cumberland counties are dramatically steeper than those further south.

Houses on their most basic level are shelter. And shelter is critical to survival in Nova Scotia: the basic weather conditions and patterns in this region haven't changed since the days when Kluskap, the Mi'kmaq Great Spirit, is said to have travelled south to find Summer and beg her to return. The maritime environment is damp and windy, characterized by howling winter gales with sleet, snow, rain and numerous freeze-thaw cycles; an unreliable spring compared to the interior of the continent; and cool, short summers. Since the only heat source until the first part of the nineteenth century was the fireplace, the fact that many early houses were small, one- or two-room buildings was a virtue. The hearth was truly central to these dwellings: it was not only the sole source of warmth but of light and of heat for cooking.

While the basic function of a house is shelter, it bears additional meanings from the time of its construction onward. An old house is a historical record, making statements

about local and regional economies, about patterns in peoples' lives, about changing technologies — saws, cooking and heating systems, wall coverings, communications –- about changing social, economic and political systems, about its inhabitants' wealth and status, about fashion. Houses illustrate changing attitudes towards intimacy and interpersonal relations, space and landscape, towards what constitutes "basic needs." It's difficult for us in the early twenty-first century to imagine surviving winter in an uninsulated eighteenth-century house like that of Simeon Perkins in Liverpool, where he had to thaw his ink to make an entry in his diary.

Through the work of archaeologists, cultural geographers, architectural and material culture historians, we know that early settlers in North America built dwellings that were very like the ones in their region of origin. They continued doing what they knew from home until new conditions caused a change. Sometimes they built with wood because the stone or brick they were accustomed to using at home wasn't available here; sometimes they were influenced by people from other regions whose different way of building was easier or produced a better result. Many of these influences and adaptations in Nova Scotia's earliest housing history have

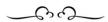

yet to be studied in great detail; nevertheless, a lot of work has been done already and can be brought together to flesh out Nova Scotia's housing story. It has been exciting to go to the libraries and discover books and articles not just about Canadian and American buildings, but specifically about Nova Scotian buildings.

The regional origins of Nova Scotian colonists suggest where to look for the roots of the province's housing history. Settlers came from the French areas of Poitou, St. Malo and Rochefort and the Basque country in the later 1600s; from the lower British Isles and Germany in the mid-1700s; from New England in the 1760s, as Planters; from Yorkshire, mainly to Cumberland County, from 1772 to 1775; from the American colonies to all parts of Nova Scotia, New Brunswick and Canada in the 1780s, as Loyalists; from the Celtic parts of the British Isles to northeastern Nova Scotia after 1780, including the migration of 20,000 Gaelic-speaking Highland Scots to Cape Breton. By 1840, the great waves of immigration were over.

The English colonists who settled Cape Cod and Nantucket in the seventeenth century came from southeastern England. They had built with wood at home in Essex and Devon, and since Massachusetts was covered in trees when they arrived, they continued using familiar building technologies and wooden house forms. Over the years they made adaptations, and when their descendants came to the Cape Sable and Barrington areas of Nova Scotia, they in turn built houses like those they knew on Cape Cod. The "Foreign Protestants" who settled in Lunenburg borrowed this one-storey vernacular design for their own houses, replacing its familiar post-and-beam framing with their own coulisse construction technique, rarely used elsewhere in colonial North America.

Technology is a major factor in housing history, largely determining what was built when. Simply producing building materials in an age of hand tools required a great deal of labour and time. Just because there were lots of trees didn't mean it was easy to create a reasonable shelter: trees don't grow in a form ready to build houses with. Even new settlers used to building with wood still had a lot of very hard work to do.

Imagine cutting down a tree with just a felling ax, then trimming its bark and branches, then smoothing and squaring the trunk into rectangular timber with a broad ax. Finally you'd be ready to make lumber from the timber. With a hand-powered pit saw you could make 100 to 200 board feet a day; with a water-powered up-and-down saw you could increase production to 500 to 1000 board feet. It wasn't until the circular rip saw, capable of producing 25,000 to 30,000 board feet per day, was developed in the 1860s that making houses became an industrial process rather than an artisanal one. Before people on the East Coast began, in the 1870s, to adopt the balloon framing system using two-by-fours and wire nails, most houses in Nova Scotia were timber-framed structures.

It mostly comes down to money. It has always taken resources — time and know-how and money — to build a house, big or small. Nova Scotia's economy has influenced the way its houses look and when and where they were built. Nova Scotia was only settled in isolated pockets until the early nineteenth century and life was a hard struggle. Many immigrants were poor and came in search of better lives. The route most people took was to acquire land for farming. The challenges were great for those who had no agricultural experience or who found themselves on uncleared or poor land. Historians point out that deporting the Acadians in 1755 damaged the Nova Scotian economy and that it didn't really recover until the 1820s. Generally speaking, most Nova Scotian fortunes have been modest.

Until the mid-1800s, few people could afford to be concerned with the style of their houses. Those few included high-level government officials, like Governor John Wentworth and Richard John Uniacke, and successful entrepreneurs who owned vessels and were involved in webs of trade and exchange in fish, timber and commodities, like Charles Ramage Prescott. As elite members of society, they wanted to express their status and wealth in visible ways. Even so, their houses are generally conservative and modest when compared to what was being built in England or the United States at the same time.

Several large Georgian Classical Vernacular houses in Lunenburg bear witness to the fact that people in the young settlement were, nevertheless, managing to build good houses in the late eighteenth and early nineteenth centuries. There are enough Greek Revival houses along Route 302 in Cumberland County to suggest that the area was quite settled in the 1840s and 1850s and that the region's farmers were prosperous enough to build substantial houses with some decorative features. The many showy Queen Annes in Amherst, New Glasgow, Truro, Yarmouth and Kentville attest to the money that was made in these towns during the last part of the nineteenth century: all were booming centres of manufacturing or industry of one kind or another. One sees a number of Craftsman houses in various towns as well, so building continued in the early decades of the 1900s.

The huge amount of time and labour it took to make lumber and forge nails in pre-industrial times helps explain the early Nova Scotian practices of adapting buildings to different functions, moving them and building additions onto existing structures. The Sinclair Inn in Annapolis Royal, now being preserved by the Historic Restoration Society, exemplifies how a structure could be renovated, altered and even relocated in order to reduce labour and materials costs. In his memoir, *Yarmouth, 1821*, James Farish refers over and over again to these practices: a school that was modified to serve as a dwelling, or sheds that were moved to new locations. An economic reason, apart from the moral one, why

the British government's decision to burn Acadian houses was a bad one was that it destroyed good building materials.

The decision also deprived us of the opportunity to study pre-1755 Acadian housing. Our current knowledge is based on archaeological excavations of two house sites in Belleisle and one in the Melanson settlement, both in the Annapolis Royal area. The evidence indicates three construction techniques: *charpente* half-timbered framing, filled either with *pièce sur pièce* (horizontal log fill) or *bousillage* (clay-rich mud and salt marsh hay) and *piquet* (vertical log construction).

How the evolution of house types is affected by a developing economy, an aspiring middle class and new technologies is a matter of practicality as well as style. People usually increased their living space by adding on rooms and raising the roof. In the process, they mimicked the layout and a few decorative features of high-style houses. They made the window arrangement regular, they centred the door. The taste for symmetry and other classical principles spread throughout the population. The result is the familiar form that we think of as the Classical Vernacular Nova Scotian house. The *Acadian Magazine* from January 1827 contains this description of the Maritime house: "built of wood, two stories high, with a pitch roof and covered with shingles." With its central hall plan, this is the most common house form in Nova Scotia.

A plain house might catch the eye because it shows off a high-style feature — the pointed window or steeply pitched roof of a Gothic Revival or the recessed front entrance of a Greek Revival. Builders and owners often altered early vernacular houses to increase space and light and to be up-to-date by adding gable-fronted wings, bay windows, verandas or kitchen ells.

During the 1840s and 1850s, the Victorian romantic sensibility began to gain force. English Georgian Classicism gave way to a taste for the Picturesque. The number of Gothic Revival, Italianate, Second Empire and Queen Anne houses across the province is clear evidence that Nova Scotians were not immune to changes in house tastes and technologies in the second half of the nineteenth century. In the post-classical period the proportions of houses change, displaying a verticality that didn't exist previously. The rectangular form may appear at first glance to be classical, as in the William D. Lawrence House in Maitland, but it's been stretched, pulled upwards. Ceilings are higher to accommodate bigger furniture. Glass is less expensive so windows get bigger. Stoves, central heating and servants make it possible to operate larger houses.

Information about new house styles and building practices became available to Nova Scotians through pattern books written for the public, through magazines, letters and travel. Americans were as susceptible as Canadians to British

tastemakers. Andrew Jackson Downing, the American who wrote the hugely influential publications, *Cottage Residences*, in 1842, and *The Architecture of Country Houses*, in 1850, had been deeply influenced by John Loudon. Loudon was a Scottish landscape gardener, architect and writer of popular books whose 1833 *Encyclopedia of Cottage, Farm, and Villa Architecture* was a potent force in the breakdown of the classical influence in Britain. Downing reproduced Loudon's material in his books.

As early as 1856 it was possible to order lithographed working drawings and printed specifications from the New York firm Cleaveland and Backus Brothers for house designs in their *Village and Farm Cottages*. The very popular *Godey's Lady's Book*, read widely in North America between 1840 and 1860, published hundreds of cottage plans in an effort "to improve the cottage architecture of our countryside."

The word "cottage" occurs frequently in both the nineteenth and twentieth centuries. There are named cottages in Nova Scotia, such as Rosebank Cottage in New Ross and Greenwood Cottage in Sherbrooke. What do these buildings have in common that makes them both "cottages"? Andrew Jackson Downing defines the cottage this way: "It is a house of limited accommodation, and above all, of very moderate size as compared with other houses.... In England, a house is often called a cottage which would here be called a villa, and the reverse, because [of] the great size of many mansions in England.... What we mean by a cottage in this country is a dwelling of small size, intended for the occupation of a family, either wholly managing the household cares itself or, at the most, with the assistance of one or two servants." The *Oxford English Dictionary* agrees with Downing, quoting an 1845 source: a cottage is "... a particular designation for small country residences and detached suburban houses, adapted to a moderate scale of living, yet with all due attention to comfort and refinement."

After 1850 the exteriors of these "small country residences" bore increasingly elaborate decoration, as woodworking machines made it possible to produce window sashes, doors and decorative woodwork such as brackets, bargeboard and finials for the picturesque nineteenth-century styles. Between 1880 and 1910 this millwork was available province-wide. The Rhodes Curry company in Amherst was the biggest producer, with mills around the province and branch offices in Sydney, New Glasgow and Halifax. The railroad made it easy to ship materials anywhere. This was a remarkable time for Nova Scotian housing: an amazing array of materials, pattern

books galore, builders at hand and a ready market. In the last decades of the 1800s, Nova Scotians aspired to a successful industrial economy. Factories produced glass, textiles, furniture and many other products. The largest Canadian steel producer of the period was in Londonderry.

But the small regional market combined with a twenty-year

recession from the 1870s through the 1890s led banks to relocate and invest elsewhere. Central Canadian manufacturers bought and closed down Nova Scotian factories. Small producers and suppliers couldn't compete with large mail-order businesses from outside the region and failed. Thousands of people left the province to make lives elsewhere as early as the 1860s and outmigration continued for decades. The population stopped growing after 1881. The Great Depression of the 1930s started ten years earlier in Nova Scotia than elsewhere.

Within this economic context, it appears that the most enduring investment made by Nova Scotians during the late nineteenth and early twentieth centuries was in housing stock. These houses are still with us, providing living spaces and heritage records. And even though the building boom slowed down in the first half of the 1900s, houses continued to be built and to evolve as they had in the preceding centuries. The dominant twentieth-century tastemaker in Nova Scotia was the United States, but British influences still remained. Nova Scotians generally followed two particular style trends during the first half of the century, the Period Revivals and the Craftsman. The post-1950 period is recent enough that we tend not to think of houses from this period as part of the housing heritage, but the fact is that many of these houses are now being renovated, and it's time to start looking at this group.

It would be fun to learn just how many houses of any particular style there are in Nova Scotia. Imagine many people doing a lot of house-gazing, comparing notes and tallying the numbers. Then we would know a lot more about Nova Scotia's housing history and heritage: what the most common styles are, how rare a particular style of house is. Houses represent an unequalled record and legacy of Nova Scotians' experiences and lifestyles.

Luckily for us all, there are people who love and appreciate many of these houses and want to care for them. But as any homeowner well knows, maintenance is a never-ending and costly fact of life. For the owner of an old house who tries to retain its authenticity of materials and appearance, the issue can be even more complicated and expensive.

Houses change over time, and trying to keep them preserved as in the past is something that even museums have difficulty accomplishing. Gowrie, in Sydney Mines, is an example of a house that has aged with dignity and spirit. Begun in the 1820s, it was added to and modernized several times to reflect the changing needs and fortune of its owners, the Archibald family. The house displays this history of change with Georgian grace, thrown a little off balance by Victorian bay windows and a complex floor plan. The house was slipping into disrepair when new owners took on the task of renovating it with great affection, energy and perseverance and adapting it so that it could survive. It now lives on as Gowrie House, an elegant inn, as important today as an example of an old house with a new life as it was a century and a half ago, when it was the home of a local businessman.

Many houses are not so fortunate. The housing legacy in Nova Scotia has suffered great losses to vinyl siding and sliding windows. Details are gone. Proportions are changed. The effect is not the same. In some towns whole districts are covered with pastel-coloured siding — but homeowners no longer have to scrape and paint, and these are understandable justifications. Other compromises are made because it is too expensive or simply impossible to find original-size building stock or people with the required skills and interest to replace deteriorated or missing elements. Owners with limited resources have to choose between restoring the exterior or making the interior habitable. Authenticity and functionality are often conflicting values.

Since 1980, the Province of Nova Scotia's *Heritage Property Act* has provided

> for the identification, designation, preservation, conservation, protection and rehabilitation of buildings, structures, streetscapes, areas and districts of historic, architectural or cultural value, in both urban and rural areas, and to encourage their continued use.

To achieve these purposes, the act affords some powers to the province and others to municipalities.

Under the act, the province established a registry of properties with provincial heritage significance. Though properties are placed on the provincial registry under the appropriate minister's authority, the act requires that an advisory council review and recommend potential heritage properties. As of May 2003, 256 properties had been placed on this Registry. Just over half of these are houses. Heritage Conservation Districts have been registered in Grand Pré, Lunenburg, Maitland, Truro and Yarmouth.

The program also administers financial grants to assist heritage property owners. When it has adequate resources, the heritage property program provides assistance to people seeking knowledge and direction about heritage buildings. It encourages networking among property owners, communities, heritage groups, architects, engineers, other levels of government and politicians.

Under the *Heritage Property Act*, municipalities are given authority to establish a registry of properties with local or regional heritage significance and to establish Heritage Conservation Districts. A number of municipalities have done so, and several have created websites featuring their heritage buildings. It's not unusual to come upon a well-maintained house in a town or the countryside and then notice that it displays a provincial or municipal heritage plaque.

In addition to being good examples of a particular style, the houses in this book were selected for a combination of reasons that include accessibility, condition and serendipity. About three-fifths of the houses may be visited, being either museums, bed-and-breakfasts, inns or parts of public institutions. The museums included in this volume are: Cole Harbour Heritage Farm Museum, Churchill House and Marine Room Museum, Cossit House, Highland Village, Knaut Rhuland House Museum, Lawrence House Museum, MacDonald House Museum, Perkins House Museum (Acacia Grove), Ross Farm Museum, Ross-Thomson House Museum, Shand House Museum, Sherbrooke Village, Uniacke Estate Museum Park, Wallace and Area Museum (Kennedy House, also known as Davison-Kennedy House). Serendipity comes from the act of house-gazing itself, from driving through the landscape and walking through neighbourhoods, looking at every house that appears! In doing so, we discovered that there are more good houses in Nova Scotia than we ever suspected.

Georgian Classical

⟨φ⟩

The dominant architectural styles of the eighteenth and early nineteenth centuries have their origins in the temples of ancient Greece and the ceremonial buildings of ancient Rome. These classical styles are known by a variety of names: Palladian (named for Andrea Palladio, an Italian architect who was hugely influential and widely copied); Georgian (named for the four kings of England who reigned between 1714 and 1830); Adams (named for the Adams brothers, British designers); Federal (the Adams style, as it was practised in the United States after the American Revolution); and Regency (the styles that evolved during the reign of the Prince Regent, George IV). The classical influence persisted in Nova Scotia for over a hundred years from the time of British settlement in the mid-eighteenth century. "Georgian Classical" is a useful general term to describe the style as it was used for houses in Nova Scotia during this period. Thereafter the classical

Opposite: With its imposing pediment supported by columns, Mount Uniacke was built to fit the ideals of a Georgian country house on an estate in the British Isles. The Uniacke Estate Museum Park is part of the Nova Scotia Museum.
Above: The portico of Government House, Halifax, is an excellent example of the Doric order, which includes the columns and the entablature they support.

vocabulary never really disappears: it gets spoken with different accents in a series of "revival" styles.

The classical orders are the five types of columns used in ancient Greek and Roman temples: Doric, Tuscan, Ionic, Corinthian and Composite. The orders were described during the Renaissance, when a grammar for their use was recovered from the writings of Roman authors and from observation and measurement of surviving ancient buildings. These discoveries were widely published throughout Europe. Each order was found to have a distinctive character, more appropriate to particular types of building than to others. For example, a Tuscan column is squatter and more robust than a slender Corinthian column. Each of the orders has its own set of proportions that enable architects to determine the size of the various elements of the building of which the column is a part.

The grandest Georgian Classical home in Nova Scotia is Government House on Barrington Street in downtown Halifax. Like many grand buildings, it was not uncontroversial: constructed in the first years of the eighteenth century as an official residence for the colonial governors, some felt the design was too extravagant. The ever-escalating cost of the sandstone building ensured that the original budget was spent with only the foundation and first-floor walls completed.

Proportion and symmetry are characteristic of the classical system, and Government House communicates these qualities clearly. Its balanced arrangement consists of a three-storey central block with smaller wings on either side. It's useful to examine the central block alone without the wings, because it is easier to imagine how the style applies to smaller, less complex houses. The façade facing the harbour, originally intended as the main entrance, has five window bays in the centre block, each separated by pilasters. Think of pilasters as flattened columns, attached to a wall; they are a useful way of expressing the particular classical order without the expense of freestanding columns. The pilasters give a rhythm to the façade, ensuring regular spacing for the windows and determining the size of the very plain entablature.

On the ground floor the joints between each stone are deeply recessed, a technique called rustication. This gives the masonry a particularly rugged and strong appearance, visually appropriate to the role of supporting the columns above. The rusticated stonework divides the façade horizontally and this horizontal emphasis is another characteristic to watch for in the classical system. The arches over the windows also contribute to this impression of strength. Window openings are so crisp and unadorned they look as though they were cut in the masonry with a laser. The contrast between the solidity of the wall and the void of the undecorated window openings is especially striking. More decoration is lavished on the entrance, a portico with freestanding Doric columns and a semicircular fanlight window over the door.

Another extraordinary classical building in the grand theme is Mount Uniacke, a country home built between 1813 and 1815. Richard John Uniacke was the attorney general of Nova Scotia, of Anglo-Irish origin, and intended his estate to be a showplace of contemporary ideals for a country house. This meant that the siting of the house and

The elegant public face of Government House (opposite), with its bow fronted wings, was originally intended as the back of the house. This Georgian Classical building (opposite and above) has a horizontal emphasis. The façade is divided into three layers: the rusticated ground floor, upper floors with bands of windows separated by pilasters and all of it topped with a hipped roof.

The garden façade of Mount Uniacke (right) looks out over a landscape carefully planned to create a picturesque effect. The semi-circular window in the pediment is echoed at ground level, above the front door.

its landscaping were as important to the intended effect as was the building itself. Today, as in Uniacke's time, the estate is approached on the original Halifax–Windsor road and the impressive garden front of the house first glimpsed across an open field. Four columns support a projecting pediment, looking like a classical temple grafted onto the house. Below the pediment is a broad terrace extending the width of the building, providing a strong horizontal base to support the "temple." This terrace is equivalent to the rusticated ground floor of Government House. At Mount Uniacke, however, only the house's foundation is stone. The rest of the structure is wooden, evidence that Uniacke was not entirely opposed to the North American way of building, though he may well have used stone could he have afforded it. Pilasters at the corners of the building echo the columns, and support an entablature as the columns do. Plain corner boards are often the only hint of columns found on less grand Georgian Classical houses.

The house was originally built with a flat roof surrounded by a balustrade, making the pediment even more prominent. This didn't shed

Nova Scotia's abundant snow and rain very well and was later covered with a hipped roof. The pediment is pierced by a huge semicircular window, a striking architectural gesture. There is a strong possibility that the house was designed by John Plaw, the first qualified English architect to practise in Nova Scotia and Prince Edward Island.

Acacia Grove in Starr's Point is another country house, built by Halifax merchant and horticulturalist Charles Ramage Prescott. The design is understated and refined but contains many clues to its classical pedigree. The house is built of soft brick made of local clay and has been painted. Window caps, sills and front steps are sandstone. A horizontal band of stone runs around the centre of the building, and another separates the foundation from the wall above: these are called string courses and are often found in masonry buildings of this style. They indicate floor level, but can also be thought of as a base

Acacia Grove, in Starrs Point, has the sense of order and balance expected of a fine Georgian Classical house. The five bays on the front are in perfect symmetry with the five on the side. Decorative elements are concentrated at the entrance (above left): a fan light over the door, columned portico and delicate cast iron railing.

supporting a row of imaginary columns. Real columns are found where expected -— at the entrance, supporting a pediment left open for a large fanlight over the door. The hipped roof has a slight curve, or bell cast, that adds to the grace of the building.

How do the homes of the wealthy and influential relate to those of

The Benjamin Knaut House, a museum in Lunenburg, shows its kinship with grander Georgian Classical houses by its horizontal stance, with a raised basement and five window bays.

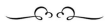

Georgian Classical ideals are quite evident in the diminutive Cossit House Museum, Sydney.

top floors of Government House. That this simple building captures the classical sense of proportion and symmetry demonstrates that its builder was style-conscious. Cossitt had grown up in Connecticut and was well educated. He would have known a classical house when he saw one.

If there were a contest for the prettiest house in Nova Scotia, Girvan Bank in Annapolis Royal would be an assured finalist and the winner on many people's score cards. There is a timelessness and confidence about the design that makes this 1817 home feel both modern and antique at the same time. The classical balance, symmetry and general sense of repose are clear. As refined as Girvan Bank is, it shows early signs that house design was headed towards a more eclectic approach. The three-part bow windows, the leisurely curve of the hipped roof extending to broad, plain eaves, and the open veranda along the house's front create a picturesque quality that is generally absent from more formal classical buildings.

people from other classes? To answer this, we have to look at the oldest surviving houses in the first settled communities, dating from the late eighteenth to the early nineteenth centuries. Look for two-storey houses with five windows and gable roofs. Decoration, if any, will be found around the door: pilasters or a small portico or porch with a fanlight and sidelights. The late eighteenth-century Benjamin Knaut House in Lunenburg is a good example. Here the basement is clearly separated from the rest of the house, stressing the horizontal feeling. Wide corner boards hint at columns. Relatively small windows with relatively plain surrounds accentuate the rhythm of solid and void.

An even more basic example of the Georgian Classical house is the Sydney home of the Anglican minister and Loyalist Rana Cossit. Although it fits more comfortably with the vernacular houses of the next chapter, the rhythm of its window openings is reminiscent of that on the

Girvan Bank in Annapolis Royal, built in 1817, has the symmetry and balance of a classical house, but it is also an early example of a taste for the Picturesque that dominated house styles for the rest of the nineteenth century.

In the Vernacular Tradition

G othic Revival, Queen Anne and other high-style houses offer lots of clues to their identities. But many buildings in the landscape say only "old house" or present a perplexing mix of messages about style. These are often the homes of "regular folks," who built their houses similar to those of their neighbours. Perhaps they worked with builders who provided some design and construction expertise, or consulted pattern books for inspiration and guidance. As artifacts or records these homes reflect their owners' resources and needs and their status in the community. Alterations record how these needs and aspirations changed over time.

"Vernacular" is a useful term to describe many of these houses, suggesting something native, indigenous or homegrown. In the world of architectural heritage, vernacular refers to

A large central chimney served fireplaces in the original two rooms of the Giles House. A later addition along the back gives the house a "saltbox" shape.

Opposite: Simeon Perkins built his house (the Perkins House Museum) in Liverpool using familiar forms and construction techniques from his native New England. When more space was needed he added a room to the left side of the house which accounts for the asymmetry of the front façade.

houses that offer local interpretations of the polite or high styles used by trained architects and by architecturally sophisticated builders. Many favourite and special Nova Scotian houses are comfortably and honourably "in the vernacular tradition."

The earliest European settlers in North America usually built their first permanent houses using the folk traditions they had learned in their former locales. Carpenters and joiners knew how to make houses the way their grandfathers had and continued to do so until new conditions suggested a change. Adaptations, like covering joints between wall boards with birch bark, responded to the climate of the New World and took advantage of local resources. By the mid-eighteenth century, when British-sponsored settlements were first established in Nova Scotia, vernacular building types had evolved in New England that were quickly adopted as suitable for ordinary people in the new colony. Many of the these settlers, or Planters, came from colonies to the south, but even when they arrived directly from Britain, as in the 1749 founding of Halifax, New England influence could still be present. Most of these new arrivals were Londoners, with no idea

The Cole Harbour Heritage Farm Museum has exposed construction details in the Giles House to show how the building has endured over the last two hundred years. A section of coulisse construction is visible above the table.

The Joseph Giles House at the Cole Harbour Heritage Farm Museum is a good place to start looking at vernacular traditions. A house can't be much simpler in form. When built around 1800, this one and one-half storey, gable-roofed house had two rooms, each with a fireplace served by a large central chimney. Above was a sleeping loft. This type of cottage is widely and not altogether accurately known as a Cape Cod, after a house form that developed along the edges of the New England coast. There are houses of the same general shape and scale, with variations in floor plan and construction, throughout Nova Scotia.

In its construction details, the Giles House follows a particular European folk building tradition. The oldest part of the house is coulisse construction, in which walls are made of squared horizontal logs slotted into channels cut into vertical corner posts. This technique is particularly associated with the European Foreign Protestants who settled Lunenburg. It was also used in New France. How do we account for this Lunenburg building practice showing up in Cole Harbour? Perhaps the historical fact that Joseph Giles bought his Cole Harbour

how to build a shelter: carpenters and prefabricated house frames were imported from Boston to get the new town under way.

The second addition Simeon Perkins made to his house was a wing off the back. The add-ons to many vernacular buildings are records of changes in the owner's resources and space requirements.

property from Jacob Conrad, a Foreign Protestant, is one part of the answer. Perhaps the physical fact that individual wall planks are numbered with Roman numerals is another. This wouldn't have been necessary unless the building components were prefabricated.

It wasn't uncommon for house frames to be made in one region and transported elsewhere.

A seven-foot extension was later built at the back of the Giles House and the roof extended over it, turning the house into what is known as a "saltbox." This additive approach was how homeowners gained more space: it was common in Nova Scotia to enlarge this type of house by adding to one end or the other. Simeon Perkins added an extension to his Liverpool house fourteen years after it was built in 1767, ending up with a front façade with two windows on one side of the door and three windows on the other. Eleven years later he added a wing to the back of the house. People have always altered their houses as need arises. With folk and vernacular houses, these additions are often casual and unselfconscious.

Eighteenth-century illustrations of Halifax show many houses with

A gambrel roof, as seen on the Jeremiah Calkin House in Grand Pré, provided more usable space on the second floor than a gable roof, as found on Simeon Perkins' house.

gable roofs with two slopes, known as a gambrel; the sort of roof that looks right on a barn. This roof shape provides more usable living space on the upper floor than does a plain gable. None of these houses have survived in Halifax, because most of them were built in the often burned and rebuilt central business district. One day, however, the authors witnessed the demolition of two buildings that abutted one another in downtown Halifax and briefly glimpsed the silhouette of a gambrel roof. One building had once shared a wall with a gambrel-roofed building that had been taken down and replaced in the nineteenth century; the newer building had encapsulated the form of

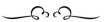

Rosebank Cottage, at Ross Farm Museum, New Ross, is similar to many eighteenth and nineteenth-century houses throughout Nova Scotia. Its functional form can be seen with many variations in height, floor plan and added decorative details around the windows and doors.

In houses like Rosebank Cottage, the large kitchen hearth was the centre of family life. By 1830 the warm glow of the cooking fire was being replaced by black cast iron stoves, and many people mourned the loss.

the older roof line. As a backhoe clawed away, the narrow trace of the two-hundred-year-old gambrel was exposed for a couple of minutes and then disappeared into a pile of rubble. Elsewhere in the province a few eighteenth- and early nineteenth-century gambrels have survived. One built by Jeremiah Calkin near Grand Pré has been restored with care. Calkin, like Simeon Perkins, moved to Nova Scotia from Connecticut in the 1760s. His house, like that of Perkins, has an asymmetrical façade, the result of being enlarged to fit a growing family.

Rosebank Cottage is the picturesque name Lieutenant William Ross gave the small house he built in 1817 in the wilderness of Lunenburg County. Ross was Irish and settled Nova Scotia's interior upland, in what is now called New Ross, with members of his disbanded regiment after the Napoleonic Wars. Like the Giles House, Rosebank uses the coulisse technique for some wall construction. Based on this evidence, it seems the new settlers got assistance from builders in the coastal settlements, who introduced their distinctive construction practice to the interior. Erecting the heavy, hand-hewn frames of houses certainly required many hands. "Raisings" were exciting affairs, and all the men and boys in a small community would turn out to help. James Farish, the nineteenth-century Yarmouth writer, remembered a common saying to the effect that a frame could not be put together "except by the aid of the lubricating fluid which was freely distributed on these occasions."

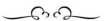

Above: The gable end of the Stewart House, Grand Pré, shows an elegant classical detail with the return of the roof at the eaves. The windows on the ground floor of the main house have a generous nine panes in the top sash and six in the bottom, although windows in other parts of the house are the more common six over six.
Left: Often the most style-conscious element of an interior was the surround of the parlour fireplace, like this finely moulded example in the Stewart House.

Rum was widely available in the young colony and was blamed for the slow progress of some settlements. Perhaps it accounts for why some houses never seem to have been quite square.

In 1818, Lord Dalhousie, the colonial governor, rode four and one-half hours on horseback over a "scarcely passable" trail to visit Edward Ross and his settlement. Dalhousie lived in Government House in Halifax, the finest Georgian house in the colony, but the Ross's "hut" shared with it the symmetry and balance that are essential to houses in the classical tradition. Although they look simple, the modest buildings of the Classical Vernacular shouldn't be underestimated. There is something about their proportions and how they fit into the landscape that is "right," in the same way that the classical orders seem so apt and timeless, reappearing century after century. One and one-half-storey buildings in the Classical Vernacular tradition continued to be built well into the nineteenth century, often with more elaborate entrances that reflected changes in floor plan allowing for a central hall. The "Cape Cod" reappeared as part of the twentieth-century Colonial Revival and has been with us ever since.

Two-storey houses of the Classical Vernacular type have a horizontal feel and a confident sense of order that makes their kinship to higher-

Stewart House door with fanlight.

style Georgian homes easy to understand. They almost always have five windows across the second floor and a central door. They are massed plan, that is, two rooms deep. The 1770s Stewart House in Grand Pré and the Lennox Tavern in Lunenburg, built around 1800, are good examples. In the Stewart House the middle bay is wider than the others to provide room for an entrance hall. A huge central chimney means the hall is narrow and the staircase small and winding. Two chimneys are more common, allowing for a variety of floor plans and hallways that extend the width of the house.

The 1784 Ross-Thomson House in Shelburne is an example of another variant of the two-storey house. The gable-roofed residence is attached to a gambrel-roofed store. The house is narrower than the Classical Vernacular form we've been discussing: the interior is only one room wide, with the kitchen in the basement. Although the entrance façade is asymmetrical, the Georgian sense of order prevails. Ross-Thomson is also interesting because its front entrance is not oriented to the street, but is set deep in an urban lot surrounded by fences and other buildings. Ordinarily the long axis of a house was parallel to the street, with the blank ends facing the ends of adjacent houses, as in Lunenburg. No doubt the mercantile Ross brothers decided it made better economic sense to have the shop front on the street, and to run the house back from the shop.

For a short time Shelburne was the largest town in British North America. Established in 1783 to relocate people who left the newly independent American colonies, within two years, there were 10,000 Loyalist residents and over 1500 buildings in the town. Most soon realized, however, that a new Boston or Philadelphia was not going to be created overnight and abandoned the community. When Lord Dalhousie visited

Opposite: The Ross-Thomson House Museum runs back from the street with the store attached to the residence. Despite the asymmetry of the window and door placements, there is a pleasing sense of balance to both buildings that is often found in vernacular buildings in the Georgian Classical tradition. The twelve-over-eight windows are unusual in Nova Scotia.

Shelburne in 1816 he estimated there were about 400 residents, with "the large houses rotten and tumbling into the once fine and broad streets, the inhabitants crawling about idle and careworn in appearance, sunk in poverty and dejected in spirit." Despite this gloomy picture, a fine collection of early buildings has survived in Shelburne to be lovingly restored.

Two-hundred-year-old houses usually have a history of style-altering renovations. The enthusiasm for bay windows and verandas in the 1880s and 1890s can disguise an eighteenth-century heart. In the Victorian era old windows were often enlarged or two small windows replaced by one large one. Many early windows were small by later standards, and the division into panes was determined by the size of glass that could be produced by the technology of the day. The

Careful restoration, as seen in the Lennox Tavern, Lunenburg, reveals details like H-L hinges on the two board doors and plain wood panelled walls.

usual window configuration is two sashes with six panes each, described as six-over-six. This form is so common today that it can be surprising to realize that there are other options, like the nine-over-six seen on the ground floor of the Stewart House and the twelve-over-eight seen on the Ross-Thomson House.

As with higher-style Georgian houses, decorative details are usually found at the front entrance of a Classical Vernacular house if they found are anywhere. Many houses have semi-circular or elliptical fanlights over the

door and pilasters supporting a pediment or entablature. Original doors have six panels and were popularly known as "Christian" doors because the top four panels define a cross. So many entrances have been replaced over

Colourful paint schemes, like the red ochre on the Lennox Tavern, were more popular before the middle of the nineteenth century, when the Greek Revival style dictated that white was the most appropriate colour for houses.

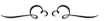

The MacQuarrie-Fox House, Iona, with its modest returns at the eaves, recessed entrance and boxy proportions, shows that its builders were influenced by the Greek Revival style.

the years, however, that when you see a finely detailed example check closely: it may date from the twentieth-century Colonial Revival.

Determining the original exterior colours of early buildings in Nova Scotia can be a challenge. The Lennox Tavern has been painted a red ochre that fits the Lunenburg enthusiasm for colour. William Moorsom, a British visitor to the town in the 1820s, remarked that "a whimsical taste has introduced the custom of painting the exterior white, red, pink and even green." When he visited Yarmouth, Moorsom noted the "large frame-houses neatly painted white" that contrasted with the "little red-coloured Acadian cottages" that he had

On the front of the Kennedy House, a community museum in Wallace, is a central projecting bay, which provides an enclosed front porch and more light and floor area in the second storey.

seen in Clare. Painting involved skills and resources that most householders probably did not have. There may well have been itinerant or community painters who understood the practical and often poisonous chemistry of oils, pigments and dryers. Many houses may have been painted rarely, if at all. Early twentieth-century black-and-white photos of Nova Scotian houses suggest this is the case. In some fishing communities, such as those along the northeast coast of Cape Breton, a person's house might be painted the same colour as their boat and with the same marine paint.

As the nineteenth century progressed, vernacular versions of many high styles became popular. Compare the MacQuarrie-Fox House, originally built in Port Hastings about 1865, with Rosebank Cottage,

about fifty years older. The newer house has the boxy feel of the Greek Revival with that style's characteristic recessed doorway and eave returns. The more horizontal Rosebank seems to sit more comfortably and securely in the landscape. Some feel that as builders moved away from traditions rooted in folk building practice and tried to emulate new styles, they lost forever the old way of seeing and sense of proportion.

Gable-fronted houses with an ell are a common sight in rural Nova Scotia. They come in all sizes and can be quite plain or more decorative, like this big farmhouse on a hill in the Middleboro area near Wallace.

As various styles and their features developed in the nineteenth century, there was much to inspire local home builders. Houses with centre gables are one of the most common vernacular variants. If the gable is broad, the influence is Georgian or Greek Revival; if the gable is pointed then it's Gothic Revival. Another popular variant, seen throughout the province, is the one and one-half-storey house with a projecting, two-storey centre bay. Found in all

Company houses for miners are strong examples of vernacular style. Built of the most available materials in the most economic way, these reconstructed houses at the Glace Bay Miners Museum (above) seem crisper and cleaner than the real thing. Also in Cape Breton, the truncated gable roof is a common feature in certain areas (right).

and one-half-storey, side-gable-roofed house, but the gable ends have been truncated or hipped, making a slope at both ends of the roof. Some claim this cuts the wind: the "*suête*," or wind from the southeast (*sud est*), is particularly strong in this region, explaining why its houses are sometimes connected to the barn by various additions. This makes it easier to care for animals in severe wind conditions that make it difficult to walk outdoors.

Along this coast there are many variations on the truncated-gable-roofed house. Some have a single, central dormer, others two dormers, symmetrically placed. The dormer roofs are often hipped, but shed dormers (having a roof with a single pitch) are also common. Often the front door is centred with a window on either side. A single central chimney is common. Sometimes it occurs in a gable-forward form, with

manner of shapes and degrees of decoration, they provided a front porch and more room and light on the upper level.

Another favourite form was the gable-fronted house with an ell at right angles. This was a popular farmhouse form and appears in all sizes from modest to grand, with either a side-hall or centre-hall plan. A veranda on the ell, often containing the kitchen, was exactly the right place for a farmer to sit after supper and watch the road. It doesn't get much more vernacular that.

Yet another homegrown house form appears frequently in the Acadian communities along the northeastern shore of Cape Breton: Cap Le Moine, Terre Noire, Grand Étang, Cheticamp. It is generally a one

The Second World War produced a big demand for workers' housing. 'Prefabs' — houses that were assembled from factory-built sections — were the expedient solution to a housing shortage. Many of them, like these in Stellarton, continue to provide economic shelter.

an ell at right angles. This truncated-roof form is also found elsewhere in the province.

A special subgroup of vernacular houses are those built for workers by their employers, the sometimes unhappy company houses. These are found in areas that were industrialized during the nineteenth and early part of the twentieth centuries, such as the coal-mining towns of Stellarton or Inverness, industrial Cape Breton and "busy" Amherst. Identical houses laid out in lines, they took many forms: row houses, semi-detached, gable- or gambrel-fronted. When we encounter groups of company houses today, their origins are not always immediately obvious.

Once owned by private individuals, there was no desire to keep them at all uniform in appearance; indeed, it may have been desirable to make them look as unlike as possible. The last big group of workers' houses were erected during the Second World War to house employees helping the war effort in communities including Halifax, Pictou, Trenton and Yarmouth. These were small, prefabricated buildings intended to be temporary, but whole streets and districts of them were upgraded to serve as permanent residences and are still in use. It is interesting to note that these small gable-roofed buildings closely resemble the Giles House, one hundred and forty years their senior.

The Scottish House

Sometimes when travelling in Nova Scotia you happen upon buildings or landscapes that evoke a feeling that you are somewhere else. A white farmhouse and red barns in the midst of forest-rimmed fields suggest Vermont, a shady street lined with big houses in the Annapolis Valley hints at small-town America. In Pictou there are echos of a Scottish town. Nowhere else in Nova Scotia is the Old World building heritage of the original settlers so clearly evident.

Opposite: Five-sided dormers are a Scottish architectural feature found in many parts of Nova Scotia.
Right: The orderly arrangement of unadorned window openings and the string course marking the second floor level place the sandstone buildings of Pictou within the Georgian Classical tradition.

Pictou was settled by Scots in several waves of immigration beginning in the late-eighteenth century and continuing into the next. The Scottish-style houses still surviving were not built by the first people who landed from boats after a perilous ocean crossing to a strange and wild land. The first years were full of hardships, but by the 1820s and 1830s merchants and tradespeople in the young town had the resources to erect the "very handsome private dwelling houses" seen by newspaper publisher Joseph Howe when he visited in 1830. Some of these houses were built of local sandstone, quarried by Scottish artisans and erected by Scots-trained masons. It's not surprising that they constructed buildings that would be at home in a Scottish High Street.

The homes are generally Georgian in form: crisp, unadorned window openings, often with a string course marking the second-floor level and a truncated gable roof. If dormers are present, they are of the distinctive five-sided Scottish variety. The same style of dormer

was popular in Halifax and along the Eastern and South shores, but it is in Pictou that they best illustrate their Scottish lineage. Another traditional Scottish feature, not often found in similar houses elsewhere in Nova Scotia, are gable-end walls that extend slightly above the roof line, called a raised parapet. Unlike houses of a similar form in Halifax the Pictou houses lack a raised basement, meaning their front doors are close to street level and appear more horizontal and solidly anchored to the ground. Like townhouses in other older settlements, Pictou houses were built right to the edge of the street. Where this edge was, however, may not always have been clear: noting the lack of well-defined streets, Howe comments that "every Building has its own particular frontal line, that very seldom agrees with that of its next door neighbour."

Occasional stone buildings crop up in the rural landscape of Pictou County and in New Glasgow, evidence of the early

The Smyth House in Port Hood has a more imposing entrance than is found on the earlier stone houses in Pictou.

days of settlement. But the stone building heritage was not sustained. There are several stone houses in Cape Breton, but only one, in Port Hood, has a sense of metropolitan style connecting it to the same heritage as those in Pictou. It is built into a bank so that the back is two and one-half storeys and the road side is only one and one-half storeys. The front door is grander that those in Pictou, with a fanlight and elegant sidelights. This house was built by Peter Smyth, a wealthy but not universally admired merchant. Smyth left Ireland as a youth and may have been trying to recreate a successful gentleman's house of his Old World memory. The house seems to have been built in the late 1850s, twenty or thirty years after the Pictonians built their stone houses. By that time the merchants of Pictou were no longer building their houses on the crowded waterfront; the town had become North American, and they were starting to imagine Italianate and Gothic villas on the large lots above the front streets, overlooking the harbour.

The raised parapet extending above the roof at the gable-ends of the Smyth House, Port Hood, is characteristic of stone houses in the Scottish tradition.

Greek Revival

⟨ɔꙮ⟩

Driving through the countryside from Amherst to Parrsboro you can see the gentle slope of a gable roof on a one and one-half storey house: a Greek Revival. Looking closely, sure enough, there is a recessed front door surrounded by sidelights with a rectangular light over the top. Wide, plain pilasters flank the door and mark the corners of the building. Broad trim runs below the roof eaves, turning the corners and making long returns on the gable ends. All the trim has been painted bright green as if to proclaim — like Zorba — "I'm Greek and proud of it." Further down the road, a two-storey version shouts its style as soon as the gable comes into view: the entablature trim boldly follows the eave return and meets the corner boards. There must have been money here in the middle of the nineteenth century and builders around the Bay of Fundy who were in the thrall of the Greek craze then rampant in the United States.

When we think of Greece today our images are often romantic: ruins of white marble temples on mountain tops, overlooking a wild and rocky landscape where heros of ancient mythology once struggled and toiled. Imagine the excitement and wonder in the early nineteenth century when Greece, isolated and remote, was rediscovered by British travellers who brought back detailed accounts of the land and accurate

Opposite and above: Gable or temple fronted houses were made popular by the Greek Revival style. The gentle slope of the roof and fully defined pediment make this house in Maitland an excellent example of this type.

drawings of its monuments. Architects were amazed to see how different classical Greek architecture was from the Roman style that came after it. Some found the Greek Doric order, which has no base and is more robust than the Roman version, crude and primitive. Robert Adam, the great British architect of the Roman classical styles, described a room decorated in the new Greek manner by one of his contemporaries as "pitifulissimo."

Despite such abuse, the Greek style gained favour among those who looked for the wellspring of classical architecture. The architectural vocabulary of ancient Greece was adopted with particular enthusiasm in the young United States. With roots in the land where democracy began and no unpleasant associations with their former colonial master, this Greek Revival was the right style for a new country entering a new century. The style became so popular that the patriotic anthem "My Country 'Tis of Thee," first sung in 1832, refers in its second verse to the "templed hills" adorned with white-painted, Greek-temple-fronted houses that remained the style of choice until the 1850s.

In Nova Scotia the Greek Revival style is not common in its purest form, but hints of it are plentiful and widespread. It has been suggested that the style was initially so associated with the republican politics of the United States that it was not entirely welcomed or trusted in the remaining British colonies, where thousands were Loyalist refugees from the American Revolutionary War. The Nova Scotian economy was also depressed after the boom years of the Napoleonic conflicts and the War of 1812. There may have been less building activity and little desire to abandon Georgian traditions that had served so well.

Probably the most striking example of a Greek Revival residence in Nova Scotia was built in 1852 for a Wolfville merchant, J.L. Brown, and is now owned by Acadia University. The vocabulary of former classical

The Brown House, Wolfville, boldly shows elements of Greek Revival style: giant Doric pilasters define the corners, while Ionic pilasters support a diminutive pediment in the centre of the front façade. The shutters and windows create dark openings against the stark white paint.

Distinctive Ionic columns or pilasters are usually a good clue that a house has Greek Revival influence.

styles remains but with a "bulked-up" feel, a bit like a body builder on steroids. Massive Doric pilasters mark the corners, and a pair of equally large Ionic pilasters support a central pediment. A shorter set of pilasters frame an entrance that is recessed into the building, another characteristic of the Greek Revival style. A rectangular transom over the door is preferred in this style, replacing the semicircular and elliptical fanlights seen on earlier buildings. A more common form of the two-storey house has three large windows across the front (in contrast to earlier five-bay houses), and a prominent door-surround with an entablature supported by pilasters.

In Lockeport there is a remarkable one and one-half-storey residence with many of the same elements as the Wolfville house, but its builder combined high-style elements with a vernacular building form. This house and an almost identical one nearby were built in the 1840s for members of the Locke merchant family and are part of Nova Scotia's first provincially registered streetscape. A small, open pediment is placed centrally in the front of a familiar side-gabled house form. Plain Doric pilasters abound, supporting the pediment and a full Doric entablature

The design of this house in Lockeport was strongly influenced by an American pattern book. Doric pilasters are used for the corner boards and around the windows and door. Below the roof line is an accurate version of a Doric entablature.

The gable fronted United Church Manse in Maitland has wooden corner "stones" and a smooth wooden façade to give the illusion of white marble.

Recessed entrances and rectangular transoms over the door are characteristic of the Greek Revival Style.

that includes triglyphs. The pilasters flank the slightly recessed door with its rectangular transom and frame all the windows on the front façade. The building may have been designed by a young builder, William Hammond, with the aid of a pattern book. He later worked in Liverpool, producing the design for one of the treasures of Greek Revival architecture in Canada, the Queens County Court House, in 1854. This building's monumental Doric columns make the pilasters on the Locke houses feel tentative and cautious.

On an ancient Greek temple you won't find dormers; Zeus did not

live over the shop. So, in order to preserve the clean silhouette and gentle roof-slope of the temple form, residents of Greek Revival one and one-half-storey houses sometimes had to suffer bedrooms with low ceilings and poor light and ventilation. To increase headroom, one simple solution was to increase the height of the short knee-wall under the eaves, providing bedrooms with a surprising amount of walking-around space. The proportions of such buildings is boxy and cubic, but a broad entablature below the eaves often helps the visual balance. Sometimes this broad band of trim includes narrow slit windows that line up with those on the first floor. These provide light and air, but usually offer a view of the ground only. They have inspired descriptive names like "prayer windows," "knee windows," "half windows" and "lie on your stomach windows." (One author emphasizes that they are not "eyebrow windows," which are curve-topped and found on roofs). A number of houses in the Barrington, Port La Tour and Coffinscroft areas use these distinctive windows, but they are more unusual elsewhere in Nova Scotia.

The Maitland house (above) and Halifax row houses (right) both show Greek Revival features in the columns, pilasters and transom light (above the doors).

Perhaps the greatest legacy of the Greek Revival style are houses with gable ends that face the street, suggesting the front of a temple. For the effect to really work the roof needs a gentle pitch like that on the Dr. Brown House in Maitland, with its complete pediment. More often the eaves simply have returns, as on the United Church Manse, also in Maitland. The front walls of both these wooden buildings are finished in smooth wood, giving the illusion of being made of white stone or marble. The Manse goes so far as to have wooden "stone" quoins at the corners. The masquerade is soon uncovered, however, as the other walls are sheathed in familiar clapboard.

The builders of these temple-fronted houses were prepared to sacrifice symmetry, placing the door off-centre to allow an entrance hall containing the stairs on one side, with the principal rooms on the other. When more space was needed it could be provided in an ell or tee. This arrangement, a gable-fronted building with a wing at right angles, had remarkable staying power and has been used ever since, without the Greek trappings and usually with a steeper roof angle.

Greek Revival houses usually did not have dormers, in order to preserve the temple silhouette. Sometimes light and ventilation for the second storey was provided by narrow slit windows located in a broad entablature just below the roof line, as in this house in Barrington.

Maitland, a product of the shipbuilding boom of the mid-nineteenth century, is as close as Nova Scotia gets to one of the white-temple-filled New England towns a short sail down the Bay of Fundy.

Because Greek Revival houses are so much more restrained than the styles that followed them, and because they have often been altered over their long lives, the style might not look particularly daring to present-day eyes. But the style opened the door, or the floodgate perhaps, for more romantic and picturesque ways of putting a house together. Chronologically the style runs from about 1820 to 1860, overlapping with the Gothic Revival and Italianate styles. Design elements from all three were often freely combined. Expect to see many "Greek Gothics," shorthand for houses with pointed centre-gables and recessed doorways framed by Doric pilasters, as you cruise through the Nova Scotia countryside.

In the United States, Greek Revival houses were universally painted white and this taste was probably shared in Nova Scotia. The village of

Gothic Revival

The Gothic Revival is a good primer for a style novice. If you see a window with a pointed top that looks like it belongs in a church, or gables that are narrow and pointed, you can shout with confidence, "Gothic Revival!" It's that easy. An arched farmhouse window glimpsed from a speeding car is all it really takes to identify this revival style, with its roots in European churches and houses of the Middle Ages. Adding to this ease of identification, Gothic Revival can be observed in one form or another in all parts of the province, it being the style used most frequently in nineteenth-century Nova Scotia. Best of all, no style gives more pleasure to the eye or feels more at home in the province's landscape. The northern origin of the original Gothic architecture accounts for some of this "rightness." Steeply sloping roofs that shed rain and snow may be functionally and visually more appropriate than those of the classical styles, whose roots stretch back to the shores of the sunny Mediterranean. A pointed gable silhouetted against the pinnacles of a native spruce forest looks right at home.

During the European Renaissance there was a break in the earlier Gothic building tradition. The

Murray Manor, Yarmouth (opposite and above)

architectural conventions of ancient Greece and Rome completely dominated high-style buildings. Yet by the 1780s, if you were strolling through the carefully contrived landscape of a grand English country house, you might be led to a vista framing the ruin of a Gothic abbey, recently fabricated of plaster and lathe, or to a pavilion with pointed arches, topped with jagged crenelations. An appetite for the romantic and picturesque encouraged late-eighteenth-century designers to draw on the rich Gothic tradition to spice up their creations. The slow but steady revival of the Gothic had begun.

There weren't many examples of this early neo-Gothic period in Nova Scotia, but a tantalizing lost example is linked to Prince Edward, Duke of Kent, who arrived in Halifax in 1794 for a six-year sojourn. Edward is generally associated with some of the province's best-loved examples of Georgian Classical architecture: Saint George's Round Church, Halifax's town clock, and the music pavilion at Princes Lodge, his country retreat. This rambling, stylish estate, built for Edward's companion Madame Julie de St. Laurent, was designed to create an exotic and romantic mood. Undoubtedly the pointed Gothic windows in the

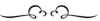

Murray Manor in Yarmouth is an early example of the Gothic influence in Nova Scotia, with its pointed ground-floor windows (left) in a classical house form. This is carried through to the panes of the bow windows (above).

kitchen wing contributed to this effect. The estate also included several Chinese-style "temples" for good measure.

British architects at the beginning of the nineteenth century were quite comfortable offering a choice of classical or Gothic decoration for the same house. Murray Manor in Yarmouth is an example of the application of Gothic features to a classical building form. Compare Murray Manor to the equally picturesque but solidly Georgian

Classical Girvan Bank: each has the low, flared hipped roof, balanced symmetrical design and low second-storey windows typical of the classical heritage. But the tall Gothic windows on Murray Manor's ground floor instantly announce that something stylistically different is at work here. Today, the house remains as distinctive and charming as it must have been when it was built, around 1820.

Adding a pointed window to a familiar house form was easy enough, and by mid-century everyone was getting into the act. By then the centre-gable house with an arched window had become the most common expression of the Gothic Revival in Nova Scotia. The jail in Sherbrooke is one example of the centre-gabled house: its pointed gable window is just one variation on a theme that ranges from small and plain to large and fanciful. Like many houses with a Gothic centre gable, the ground floor of the jail retains classical decoration around the door-way, and the ground-floor windows are square topped. Strip away the gable, and the basic classical house form remains, so there was no great change in building techniques required. If a builder or owner was wary of being too dramatic, the centre gable could be wide and low, echoing the general proportions of a classical temple pediment. To be true to the style, however, the gable should be tall and narrow, emphasizing the vertical feeling that is fundamental to the Gothic.

Centre gables vary in the pitch of slope and in the design of the window. This decorative Gothic window from in the jail in Sherbrooke Village, home to four cells as well as the jailer and his family.

As the style evolved, interpretations of medieval forms and structural features became more inventive, extreme and picturesque. Gables became narrower and steeper, double and triple gables became more common, conveniently providing light and headroom to the second floor. Along with pointed windows and gables, other Gothic elements — drip-moulds, pinnacles, finials, bays, elegant tracery — were used more widely and in various combinations, creating richer and more vertical effects. The purest expression of the style was in mid-nineteenth-century church construction. You can hone your Gothic understanding by studying the marvellous array of Anglican churches found throughout the province, the legacy of Church of England advocates seeking a return to the compositional principles of the twelfth to fourteenth centuries.

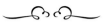

Greenwood Cottage in Sherbrooke Village is like a catalogue of Gothic Revival design elements: the windows are topped with the distinctive hood called a drip-mould; while bargeboards — the lacy, extravagant woodwork also known as gingerbread — hangs from the eaves and gables. This particular bargeboard design also shows up on other houses in the area. Finials and pendants from the peaks and corners of gable- and dormer-roofs are often the first bits of decoration to disappear.

Although the style has its roots in European masonry architecture of the Middle Ages, in Nova Scotian homes the Gothic is almost always expressed in wood. Decorative and structural elements could all be reproduced in wood, including the imitation carved-stone tracery known as bargeboard, the lacy, often extravagant woodwork that hangs from eaves and gables. Greenwood Cottage, just up the street from the jail in Sherbrooke, is an example of a home that was built completely in the Gothic Revival style: steep roof, pointed gables and dormers, drip-moulds, arched windows, projecting bay and bargeboards. Finials and pendants at the corners of the gables are the finishing touches to a house that was outstanding when built in 1871, a perfect "monster house" for a prominent businessman. The inspiration probably came from a pattern book, as there is an identical house in Pictou (likewise built for a merchant), and the distinctive bay design turns up in Maitland as well.

The name most associated with the Gothic Revival in North

The Dickie House is a great example of just how Gothic a home can be. Vertical and picturesque effects are achieved through the steeply pitched roof, the board-and-batten cladding, the ornamental veranda posts complemented by the wooden tracery of bargeboard and diagonal battens under the bracketed bay.

America is Andrew Jackson Downing. Before his death in 1852, this American tastemaker published books and articles that popularized the Gothic and stressed the style's suitability for rural homes. Downing would have been pleased with the house Maitland carpenter Thomas Dickie built for himself. It is the ultimate translation of the Gothic style into wood. The cladding is a Downing favorite, board-and-batten — wide vertical boards with narrow battens covering the joints between them. When this technique is used for residences they are almost always Gothic Revival. The house's "L"-shaped footprint has an asymmetry that distinguishes it from the styles that came before.

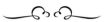

Gothic gables and windows increased the light and headroom on the second floor, as this Margaree Forks house demonstrates with great charm.

The elaborately decorative woodwork that ornaments Gothic Revival buildings was made possible by advances in woodworking technology: scroll saws and jigsaws that allowed woodwork to become as ornate as imagination and resources would allow. Steam-powered sawmills appeared in most towns to feed consumer demand. As the first style to take advantage of the freedom this new technology provided, the Gothic Revival prepared the market for buildings with ample surface decoration, complex silhouettes and the indulgence of every decorative excess that could be imagined.

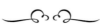

Small farm houses with a plain centre gable are a familiar sight throughout Nova Scotia. They don't get much plainer than the 1850s MacDonald House Museum, with its square-topped windows overlooking Lake Ainslie.

Italianate

〰️

Italy has hugely influenced Western culture. The Western heritage of art, music, science and literature owes great debts to Leonardo, Galileo, Dante, Vivaldi and their compatriots. Despite this, "Italian influence" is probably not foremost in our minds when we travel through the quiet towns and villages of Nova Scotia, or walk through Halifax's old business district. But if we look a little closer at that house with the arched windows and the low-pitched roof — aren't there hints of a villa nestled in the Italian countryside? And those commercial buildings with overhanging cornices and richly decorated window surrounds — isn't there some kinship to the merchant palaces of Venice?

The architectural styles of the 1850s to 1880s offer the key to deciphering these clues. When architectural tastes in Britain and North America started to demand something more decorated and exuberant than the classical tradition, styles derived from the Italian Renaissance gained popularity. These Italianate styles were popular during the same time that the Gothic Revival was in full swing. The trendsetting Andrew Jackson Downing included designs for both Italianate and Gothic styles in his popular and influential mid-nineteenth-century books.

One form of the Italianate took its influence from country villas. The Cedars (Churchill House) in Hantsport displays the connection: broad eaves supported by brackets could shade the walls from intense Tuscan sun. The low-pitched roof is apparently designed to shed Mediterranean quantities of snow. The asymmetrical plan is ordered and balanced. This house was built by a prominent shipbuilding family, the Churchills, around 1860. It was planned with care and was clearly intended to be a showpiece inside and out.

Above: The Cedars (Churchill House Museum), Hantsport, shows the low-pitched roof and the brackets at the eaves. Opposite: The front façade of the William D. Lawrence House Museum, Maitland, is unmistakably Italian in its origins.

In contrast to the view on page 59, this side of the Cedars is more complex and still true to its Italian roots, complete with the belvedere and balustrade.

On the roof is a little structure called a belvedere (meaning literally "good view"), a common decorative element on Italianate country houses that provides a panoramic view of surroundings. A popular term for this feature, surrounded by a little balustrade, is a "widow's walk" —

a place where the wife of a shipwrecked seafarer could forlornly and vainly survey the horizon, watching for his return.

A more common Italianate form is a big, squarish building with a low hipped roof, often originally topped with a belvedere. Yarmouth has a number of these grand houses, built during the prosperous decades at the end of the nineteenth century, when the town was world renowned for its shipping fleet. The Guest-Lovitt House is an imposing example. Its projecting bays with arch-topped windows on the ground floor, and paired windows with dramatic bracketed hoods are characteristic of the style. The narrowness of the windows extenuates the vertical qualities of a building that is already tall. Moulded panels between paired brackets at the extended eaves add to the richness of the visual effect. Often this type

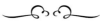

of building has lost its belvedere and other features, particularly at roof level. This had in fact happened to the Guest-Lovitt House, but a newly built belvedere has had an amazing effect in restoring its grandeur.

Another variation of the Italianate is a two-storey building with shallow projecting centre bays. Hillsdale in Annapolis Royal is an example. Here the bay has a low-pitched gable roof with dramatic returns, but a variety of detail can be

The big square Italianate buildings, like the Guest-Lovitt House, Yarmouth, lend themselves to rich ornamentation.

Hillsdale shows how the basic gable house could be transformed by Italianate elements.

seen in other examples. A pair of arched windows capped with a moulded arch is a frequently seen arrangement. Hillsdale also is a good example of the variations in window caps used in Italianate residences: the drip-moulds are similar to those on Gothic Revival houses, and the hoods supported by brackets are also characteristic.

The original Italian buildings that inspired this style were made of stone or stuccoed brick, so it is interesting to see how effectively and engagingly the style translated into wooden construction. A sandstone and stucco Italianate house on Tobin Street in Halifax offers a useful comparison to Hillsdale. The paired windows with bracketed caps are

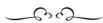

that Italianate buildings should be painted in stone colours, and he was particularly disappointed to see Italianate or Gothic buildings painted white. The swooping bell-cast roof on the Tobin Street building is an interesting transition between the gentle slope of a Georgian hipped roof and the more vertical mansard roofs that would soon gain popularity.

In Nova Scotia's northern climate, an enclosed storm porch is a common and functional addition to a house. It provides an airlock, protecting the inside of the house from extremes of weather — helping to keep cold air out in winter and the interior cool in summer. In Halifax there is a much-appreciated tradition of enclosed porches dating back to the eighteenth century, but many of the surviving examples have Italianate styling. Elsewhere in North America, Italianate houses often had open porches or verandas centred on the front door and supported

Above: This Halifax house is one of the few Nova Scotian examples of the Italianate style built of masonry. Right: Storm porches with Italianate detailing are a distinctive Halifax feature.

quite similar. The centre windows are different, but each receives special emphasis. The cornerstones, or quoins, on the masonry building provide the same sort of visual contrast as do the corner boards on the wooden residence. The masonry building is also a reminder that Downing felt

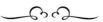

Lawrence House is a more restrained version of the Italianate Style, identified particularly by the use of brackets at the eaves. The covered passageway at the rear of the house led to the outdoor toilet.

brackets and carvings create a lively streetscape.

A more restrained relative of the Italianate is called the Bracketed style, basically the familiar gable house form adorned with brackets. At first glance, the William D. Lawrence House in Maitland looks like just another big white building with little to distinguish it. Lawrence was a determined opponent of Canadian Confederation, who built British North America's largest full-rigged wooden ship in his shipyard in front of this house. The house did matter. It's sited on top of a rise and commands a view of

by highly decorated columns, as seen on Hillsdale. The Tobin Street house's enclosed porch exploits the decorative potential of this idea, making it functional in the Nova Scotia climate. In Halifax these porches usually have a side entry. Arched windows and plentiful brackets affirm connection to the Italianate. When clustered together, as on Tower Road in Halifax, these porches with their associated bays,

Cobequid Bay and the village of Maitland. As we approach the house it becomes clear that it is massive compared to five-windowed Georgian Classical or three-windowed Greek Revival houses. The chief clue to its Italianate heritage are the brackets, one of the house's few decorative elements, essential visual support for the eaves. The eave returns also have an Italianate generosity. The windows are square topped and

W.D. Lawrence sited his large house in a commanding position on the edge of Maitland. The cast iron cresting on the roof of the porch adds some complexity to an otherwise restrained composition.

feature hints at the gradual progress of indoor plumbing during this period, as the house also has a separate bathroom with a tub and basin. For winter, the house has wood-framed storm windows and a plain storm door, reminding us that modern technologies have relieved us of the ritual preparations for winter, such as banking the foundation of a house with eel grass or sawdust to keep out winter drafts.

Unless encountered in its purest form, the Italianate is not the easiest style to recognize because it shares traits with other styles. As it waned as a high-style form, its influence continued at the end of the nineteenth century in the many flat-roofed houses with bays and brackets that share some Italianate attributes. If the style is executed well, there is no question as to its identity; but if the builder mixed styles, or included idiosyncratic decorative features, then some visual detective work may be required. On the other hand, there are many buildings that at first glance suggest no particular style, other than that "there's a bit of an Italianate feel" to them, and sometimes this gives a useful clue to the intent of the builder.

It is at this point in our architectural history that the reader who is vaguely conscious of architectural styles will say the buildings start looking "Victorian." Many of the famous, lavishly decorated and rainbow-hued "painted ladies" of San Francisco are in fact Italianate, with an over-the-top exuberance only hinted at in Nova Scotia.

capped with simple mouldings. The storm porch is side entry, but can be entered from either side; the curve of the steps giving it a nautical flair. The porch is capped with cast-iron cresting that enhances the vertical effect, even if the pattern of tiny trefoils would be more appropriate on a Gothic Revival house.

One of the charming features of Lawrence House is the two-cubicle privy reached from the back of the house by a covered walkway. This

Second Empire Style

Second Empire-style houses in Nova Scotia vary wildly in size, quantity of decoration and visual impact, yet the style is always easy to identify. What all Second Empire houses have in common is some form of mansard roof, named for François Mansart, a French architect of the seventeenth century. The origin of the style, too, is French, derived from the massive building projects that shaped Paris during the reign of Napoleon III (1852–1870), a period known as the Second Empire. Popular international exhibitions held in Paris in 1855 and 1867 brought Napoleon's building projects to the attention of architects in Britain and North America, and they quickly recognized the potential of the style. Nova Scotians also attended the 1867 Paris Exhibition: they were so proud of the exhibits they took that when the collection returned it formed the nucleus of a new provincial museum.

The mansard roof has a double slope, with the curved, lower slope steeper than the upper. The description sounds like a gambrel, but in practice they are usually not difficult to tell apart. Often the upper roof is almost flat; at other times it appears the builder was not totally ready to embrace the style, constructing the upper roof as a steeply pitched hip. The practical benefit of the mansard is that it adds a full, usable floor to the house. The exterior decoration is of classical or renaissance origin, and the style shares many traits with the Italianate and Bracketed styles. The mansard roof always contains dormers and these come in many forms: gables, pediments and arches of all shapes and sizes. Flat-topped windows are often capped with bracketed hoods; arched windows have a variety of surrounds. Segmental arched (slightly rounded) window openings are common. Expect also three-

The contrasting size of these Maitland houses (opposite and above) and the different decorative treatments illustrate that Second Empire is adaptable. The common element is the distinctive mansard roof.

The treatment of the windows is one of a number of Second Empire features that make the Queen Anne Inn in Annapolis Royal so picturesque. They have a different shape and decoration on each storey.

sided and box-bay windows that can be one or two storeys tall.

Second Empire style was particularly suited to large public buildings, and in the 1870s Nova Scotia followed a North American trend by using the style for substantial buildings, including the Normal School in Truro and the impressive north-end Halifax railway station, destroyed in the 1917 explosion. The Second Empire style could be adapted to residences for small town lots or large suburban estates. An example of a grand house with room to breathe is the Queen Anne Inn in Annapolis Royal, built in 1865. Private houses in Nova Scotia are rarely this large, and it's not surprising that, although built as a home, it has been used as a hotel and for other institutional purposes for over a hundred years. Its mansard is elegant, with a gentle curve broken by an extra cornice that ties into the dormers. Second Empire buildings often have a vertical emphasis that draws the eye upward to a central tower, as is the case here. The mansard on the tower describes a different curve and is capped with an odd little roof that swoops up to a finial. Each floor has windows of a different shape. There are large pairs of brackets at the eaves, and even larger brackets support a little balcony in the middle of the tower.

The Captain William Douglas House in Maitland uses the same general approach as the Queen Anne Inn but with a more compact, vernacular effect. The mansard describes a simpler curve and is used only on the front and back of the house. The main façade ripples with box bays that support dormers on either side of a central tower. Small roofs at the eaves cut the bays and the tower visually, making the house feel less vertical. Again, the roof on the tower has a convex shape contrasting with the concave shape of the main roof. The tower is topped with a cast-iron cresting that provides some upward thrust.

The composition of the Captain William Douglas house, Maitland, is similar to that of the Queen Anne Inn but the simpler curve of the roof and the fact that it is used only on the front and back creates a vernacular effect. Note the concave roof of the house and the convex curve on the tower's roof.

Crestings like this were common on Second Empire buildings and could be found on porches and verandas or even along the complete roof line, as was formerly the case at the Queen Anne Inn. Exposed to extremes of weather and difficult to reach, they are not easy to maintain: crestings are often the first decorative detail on these buildings to disappear.

By the 1880s many modest Second Empire houses were being built in the new suburbs of Halifax and in towns throughout the province.

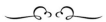

The presence of mansard roofs is, in fact, a good clue when guessing the date when development took place in a district. A small house on Welsford Street in Halifax shows how effectively the style could be scaled down and still retain its essence. Often houses of this size will have a bay window, sometimes with a bay dormer above it.

When originally built, the lower slopes of most mansards in Nova Scotia were covered with wooden shingles, sometimes with a horizontal band of decorative, shaped shingles running across the centre. This was a reminder that the mansard roof was hung with slate shingles in different patterns and colours in many areas of the world, greatly enhancing the decorative effect of these buildings. Slates were used on at least some of the big two and one-half-storey townhouses in Halifax, but most have been replaced with asphalt shingles.

At the end of the nineteenth century, adding a mansard roof was a popular way of modernizing an older gable-roofed house while gaining more useable space. Evidence of this type of renovation can be obvious in a stone or brick building, because it was difficult to match the existing masonry in the side wall and thereby hide the shape of the old gable. There are at least half a dozen early nineteenth-century masonry buildings in Halifax and Pictou that show this kind of "improvement," so it may be assumed that many wooden buildings received the same treatment. Renovated masonry houses were usually Georgian Classical to start with, and the forced marriage of styles is usually an uncomfortable one. In the 1970s, nearly one hundred years after the Second Empire style lost steam, little mansards were commonly grafted onto existing service stations and fast-food outlets to make them look friendlier. It still wasn't successful.

Left: Cast iron cresting like this was a common feature on Second Empire buildings. Its out-of-easy-reach location and the extremes of Nova Scotian weather conspired to eliminate most crestings. Twentieth-century standard window sizes and shapes make for a less-than-happy storm window solution.
Right: These neighbours on a Halifax street suggest a building date circa 1880, when many modest Second Empire houses were built in the new suburbs of Halifax and in towns across the province.

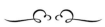

The Halifax House

The history of Halifax's growth is preserved in its street plan. The original 1749 settlement, crammed inside a wooden palisade, is still evident in the tight grid of narrow streets arranged around an open square, the Grand Parade. Fortified Citadel Hill towers over the old town, and together with a broad band of common lands effectively barred business and residential expansion away from the harbour until the advent of the street car. The first roads away from the town site ambled through the countryside, the road to Windsor becoming Windsor Street and the road to the military fortifications at Point Pleasant becoming Tower Road. By the 1860s the business district was consolidated along the streets of the original town site. A series of fires helped clear blocks of old wooden buildings,

Opposite: Halifax Box House on Jubilee Road.
Above: Pryor Terrace houses on Hollis Street.

which were replaced with Italianate-style shops and warehouses built of "fireproof" stone, brick and iron. To meet the needs of a growing population, new suburbs were laid out between existing roads on either side of the business district, land that had formerly been farms and estates.

Houses of various types appeared on these new streets, but two successive forms had remarkable popularity and longevity. The first can be called the "Halifax Big House," and was followed by a smaller form which has been called the "Halifax Box." Variations of both types were built in such large numbers that they are one reason for the special architectural character of Halifax.

The roots of the Big House lie firmly in the Georgian Classical tradition, with its emphasis on proportion and balance. The Pryor Terrace row houses, built about 1820,

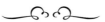

Pryor Terrace (Hollis Street) displays the characteristics of a typical Big House: each unit is three windows wide, has an elevated basement, and a five-sided dormer. Its Georgian Classical heritage is evident in the rusticated granite basements, smooth sandstone walls with crisp window openings and the string courses indicating floor levels.

A row of Big Houses on Morris Street is dominated by distinctive five sided dormers and finished in shingles.

sandstone with a rusticated granite foundation; string courses at the foundation and second floor stress the strong horizontal lines traced by the windows and cornice.

The roof is a truncated gable, meaning that instead of rising to a point the centre of the roof is flat. Huge chimneys with flues for four or more fireplaces run the full width of the flat section on both sides. The basement contained the kitchen and storerooms, and the elevated walls allowed for a comfortable ceiling

exhibit all the essential elements of the form at the time when it was gaining acceptance. Each of the three townhouses is three bays wide; an elevated basement makes the house extra tall, requiring a short flight of steps to reach the off-centre front doors. Each is built of smooth height and good-sized windows for light. Cooking was still done on a large, open hearth until about the 1830s, as cast-iron stoves gradually won acceptance. Until the 1860s most of these houses had five-sided Scottish dormers, providing a bright and roomy third floor. This attic

This house on Barrington Street was given a Mansard roof.

could be used as bedrooms for children or for servants. Middle-class families usually required a servant or two to operate such a house efficiently.

Big Houses were built in all the popular building materials — wood, brick, sandstone, even granite. The plentiful, but not particularly attractive, local ironstone was always used for the side walls of homes, with façades built of more expensive cut sandstone and granite. Even houses with wooden fronts sometimes had side walls of ironstone or lesser-quality brick to provide protection against the ever-present danger of spreading fire. Many of these houses once had fireproof slate roofs, but the lack of a continuous local tradition of

This Morris Street house still shows the Big House form but it has been shrunk to a storey-and-a-half.

using and maintaining slate has meant that virtually all have been replaced with modern roofing materials.

These Big Houses are urban structures, built right to the sidewalk line on narrow lots. There are a number of terraces of row houses, but free-standing buildings built close together are more common. These are not small houses. The principal rooms can have very high ceilings (3.5 metres from floor to ceiling) and the second-floor rooms are equally high. Even the third-floor rooms can seem generous by today's standards. There are a number of one and one-half-storey versions of the Big House, exhibiting the solid, "chunky" feel of the bigger Bigs.

For forty years Big Houses continued to be built without much change. The Greek Revival was acknowledged by plain, broad pilasters flanking slightly recessed doorways and on wooden storm porches. Gradually the houses lost some of the Georgian string courses and

By the 1860s and 70s contractors were dressing up the Big House form with Italianate and Second Empire details as seen on this brick house.

Two-storey window bays and small open verandas add complexity to the front of Halifax Boxes.

rusticated basements, and the windows got larger and were dressed up with a variety of brackets, caps and mouldings. The ever-popular five-sided dormer remained a reliable hallmark that allows these buildings to be identified quickly and accurately.

By the 1850s and 1860s the building trades in Halifax had developed sufficiently that master builders, employing a work force comprising all the construction trades, were buying building lots and constructing houses on speculation as well as by contract. These builders, who often advertised themselves as architects as well, began erecting buildings with details that reflected the international styles of the day. The exuberant final manifestation of the Big House in the 1870s and 1880s incorporated elements of the Second Empire and Italianate styles. The essence of the Big House endures under a bell-cast or a mansard roof, behind one- or two-storey bay windows festooned with brackets. Gone forever were the five-sided dormers, replaced by designs better suited to more highly decorated styles. Even some of the original Georgian-style Big Houses were modernized with a mansard roof. Evidence of some of these renovations can be seen preserved in the stone work of the side walls of several houses. As an ultimate indignity, when Big Houses were turned into flats and rooming houses, some acquired flat roofs when a floor was either added or removed.

As new suburbs developed in the last twenty years of the nineteenth century, a new dominant house form evolved to fit changing needs and life styles. A present-day resident of one of these houses calls hers a "Halifax Box," which is descriptive if not particularly complimentary. They are flat-roofed, boxy two-storey houses. The front façade usually has a one- or two-storey bay window on one side and the door on the other. The quality of decoration can vary from plain to elaborate. The whole repertoire of products available from woodworking factories — spindlework, brackets, decorative shingles, turned veranda posts, balusters — could be used. In practice, however, the decoration of most of these houses is relatively restrained. Some of the design vocabulary is Italianate and Second Empire, but in the end the houses are probably neither, just a good solution to the need for a versatile house on a compact urban lot.

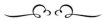

Inside the Box, the kitchen moved upstairs out of the basement, which as a result didn't need to be so high, being the new home for the furnace, coal bins, and maybe a hundred pounds of potatoes and a barrel of apples. If more living space was needed, the house could just keep expanding backward. It isn't unusual to have double parlours, a dining room and a kitchen all in a line connected by a long, often dark, hall. This would be a grand version of the Box, with fancy mantelpieces and deep plaster mouldings in the front room. There were also workers' versions of the Box. In photos taken after the 1917 explosion that flattened a large section of working-class Halifax, examples of these houses can be seen with their walls folded out and window openings gaping. When new streets were laid out to reconstruct the north end of the city, the houses were built in styles more attuned to the new century that had greeted Halifax with such a large and very tragic bang.

The Halifax Box house in its plainest form has an almost flat roof. This Jubilee Road example is decorated with brackets and rows of scalloped shingles.

Lunenburg Bump Houses

Lunenburg is special. So special that it was declared a World Heritage Site in 1995, putting it in the same fraternity as Quebec City and the pyramids of Egypt. This designation from the United Nations Educational, Scientific and Cultural Organization (UNESCO) recognized Lunenburg as "the best surviving example of a planned British colonial settlement in North America," and its inhabitants were praised for having safeguarded their community's identity by preserving its wooden architecture. Among Lunenburg's many architectural treasures is a group of buildings that combine elements of several styles in a unique and distinctive local manner.

Times were troubled when settlers began building Lunenburg in 1753, so a compact street grid was laid out to help make the town

Opposite and above: The distinctive and picturesque dormers and bays that adorn many houses in the town of Lunenburg and elsewhere in the county have acquired the name "Lunenburg Bumps." The Augustus Wolff House, built in 1888, has been carefully painted to show the ornate woodwork.

defensible against attack. Two hundred and fifty years later these same narrow streets fill each summer with a friendly invasion, as thousands of people come to experience the town's charm. These invaders throng the waterfront, made famous by the town's offshore fishing fleet, and climb the steep streets from the harbour to marvel at the tightly packed collection of houses dating mostly from the eighteenth to the beginning of the twentieth centuries. But it is the many buildings constructed or modernized between about 1870 and 1900 that are particularly astonishing. Many are adorned with picturesque dormers and bays that have acquired the not particularly attractive name "Lunenburg Bumps."

Until the 1870s Lunenburg's houses were strongly rooted in the classical tradition. The town still

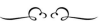

Opposite: The Morash House, with its 3-tiered "bumps," is one of the most exuberant of the Lunenburg treasures. This is a hybrid offspring of five-sided Scottish dormers mated with Second Empire and Italianate elements, with an occasional touch of Gothic Revival thrown in for good measure.
Right: The Zwicker house was a flat-fronted five-bay Classical Vernacular house that was transformed by a "Bump" renovation.

contains simple "Capes," gambrel-roofed homes and well-proportioned five-bay houses that date from the first century of settlement. By the mid-nineteenth century, five-sided dormers were commonly adopted as an attractive way to increase light and space on the top floor while visually "bulking up" the mass of a classically styled house. These dormers were probably added to existing buildings as well as incorporated into new construction. Lunenburg Bumps are the offspring of plain, five-sided Scottish dormers mated with French Second Empire

and Italianate elements, with an occasional touch of Gothic Revival decoration thrown in for good measure. The resulting hybrids are common in Lunenburg County but not elsewhere in the province.

The Augustus Wolff House demonstrates how the hybrid was created. The two small dormers still clearly show their five-sided heritage, but are dressed up with arched windows, brackets and a peculiar roof. The centre bump is another of these dormers, scaled up and positioned lower on the roof to increase the floor area of the second floor, and to provide a roof for a small porch on the ground floor.

The ultimate expression of the Lunenburg Bump House is the Morash House, built in 1888. The façade is symmetrical and dominated by a three-storey central bay. On either side are five-sided dormers that project beyond and extend below the roof line. The round-topped windows and door with sidelights are capped with heavy curved mouldings, and the flat-topped windows have projecting hoods supported by brackets. Bell-cast roofs sprout from the dormers and the central bay, only to be interrupted by bands of moulding. Substantial corner boards and a liberal scattering of brackets complete the picture. The effect is spirited and complex, as would be expected from this period. If the arch-topped windows and door were seen in isolation, it might seem the parentage was Italianate or Second Empire. The roofs on the dormers also seem to share some genes with a Second Empire mansard, but the proportions are all wrong. And the dormers have moved so far forward that they need brackets for support. This particular feature appears over the front door of many Lunenburg houses. Viewed from the gable end the Morash House is remarkably conventional, with corner boards and eave returns that would look comfortable on a Greek Revival house.

The Zwicker House is an example of an existing Classical Vernacular building, modernized. It began its days as a straightforward

Old Town Lunenburg's compact street grid means that many houses are right on the sidewalk, not leaving much room for a front porch. Often a bump overhangs the front door, affording some weather protection as you come and go, and providing excellent views up and down the street.

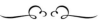
floor were more in proportion with the substantial Victorian furniture of the day. A central bay, with many of the elements seen on the Morash House was "bumped" out through the front, and the dormer rebuilt and repositioned to cap it. Imagine how different the house would have felt with the convenience of a front porch and more room and light on the second floor.

Traditional Lunenburgers are noted for their distinctive accent and strong sense of independence, and their houses reflect these traits. One can conjecture that local builders at the end of the nineteenth century were familiar with current architectural designs in pattern books and magazines, and from first-hand experience with new buildings on trips to Halifax and New England. They offered their own interpretations of these designs, enhanced by some of the same creativity that is found in Lunenburg County folk art and antique furniture. The entrepreneurs whose fishing and shipbuilding businesses fuelled the local economy were very competitive, and it's not hard to imagine there was also some

The interior of the Zwicker Inn is flooded with daylight from the front windows.

competition to see who could produce the most impressive Bump.

For those just starting to sort out architectural styles, the visual extravagance of these Bump Houses can overwhelm. On the other hand, by systematically touring the streets and seeing one amazing house after another, similarities and differences among the various approaches to the Bump begin to sink in, giving rise to a feeling of discovery and insight.

flat-fronted, five-bay house with a hipped roof, which later acquired a plain five-sided dormer. A renovation, probably in the 1870s, completely transformed the building. Pairs of small window openings were filled in and replaced by larger, single openings with bracketed and decorated hoods. The larger windows in the formal rooms of the first

Queen Anne

Getting to know the decorative and exuberant Queen Annes is an adventure. Combining a regard for composition and a delight in ornamentation, the Queen Anne attracts and satisfies the eye with its visual complexity. It was the Victorians, after all, with their romantic sensibility and taste for the picturesque, who built these houses. Popular in the 1880s, 1890s and the first decade of the 1900s, the style appealed to the burgeoning, prosperous middle classes in England and in Canada who were looking for affordable houses that were also showy. Americans took to the style after seeing British examples in Philadelphia at the Centennial Exhibition in 1876. The style coincided with and was perhaps encouraged by economic successes, technological developments and an expansionist mentality that characterized the times in all three countries.

The Queen Anne style began with a house designed in the 1860s by British architect Richard

Opposite: The Regent, Amherst, has suggestions of Gothic influence in its subtle composition.

Norman Shaw. This was during the period when many British Victorians considered the Gothic to be the one and only true architectural style. Shaw's dramatic stylistic departure was a house that combined renaissance details, borrowed from eighteenth-century English classical buildings, with details from English buildings that came before: medieval, Tudor, Elizabethan and Jacobean buildings that spanned the twelfth to the early eighteenth centuries.

The new style allowed infinite variation in ornamentation, floor plans, roof shapes and window shapes. This complexity was possible with new building technology: the light, balloon framing system of two-by-fours joined only by nails; all manner of decorative woodwork produced by steam-powered woodworking machines; reliably weather-proof brick produced with hydraulic presses. In Nova Scotia, as in New England, the style was usually built in wood, although brick predominated in England and some parts of North America.

Queen Annes occur throughout Nova Scotia and are generally easy to recognize. They

Verandas are only one of the many features that distinguish the Queen Anne style. Many examples have dynamic roof lines, a tower, a three-part Palladian window and are generally picturesque. These Queen Annes in Amherst (opposite), Truro (left) and Comeauville (above) ask for a second or third look at the complexity of shapes and decorative elements.

share characteristic features, even though no two are exactly alike. A Queen Anne is always irregular or asymmetrical in form; usually big and tall; capped with a dynamic roofscape of gables and steep roof pitches to evoke a medieval quality. Roofs are often hipped, with one or more lower cross gables. Some have cross-gabled roofs, others a full-width gable that dominates the front façade, while on others the gables are mere dormers. Often, but not always, the houses have towers, usually round, sometimes polygonal, rarely square. Square towers are usually found in the Italianate Style. A Queen Anne usually has at least one veranda.

The list of family characteristics goes on: wall surfaces are as dynamic as the roof line, never flat for very long; bays, dormers, towers and verandas push outwards and create spaces in between. Despite the thrusting and pushing, a Queen Anne is as much a polite classicist as a fanciful medievalist. Horizontal effects are created through a combination of three-part Palladian windows, string courses and variations in exterior surfaces. The essential classical quality that every Queen Anne strives for is a sense of balance, within its picturesque composition. A Queen Anne that conforms to the standards of the style looks balanced on all sides but has a different composition on at least two of them.

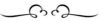

The Bishop's Residence, Yarmouth, with its many forms of wooden ornamentation, is a particular mode of Queen Anne known as spindlework. It combines turned elements, different types of wooden cladding, variations in shingle patterns, corner boards, barge board, trusses, brackets and appliqués.

The Bishop's Residence in Yarmouth illustrates how exterior decoration works with building elements in a well-composed Queen Anne. The house, built in 1892, offers two façades to the viewer. A round two-storey corner tower is a central element. When observed from the front Park Street façade, it works with the front and side gables to produce a vertical, and Gothic, effect. It plays the role of a bay window on the second floor while it rises to distinction as a third-floor look-out, resolved in a witch-cap roof. There is no expanse of flat wall surface on this house. The ground-floor bay window on the gable front moves forward decisively, in concert with the veranda it supports on the

It was possible to build wooden houses like this in the late 1800s because of innovative technologies that included steam power, the circular rip saw, balloon framing and woodworking machinery.

second storey above. The veranda has its own small gable roof to balance the composition. Around the corner on the Cliff Street façade, some of the same elements are in a satisfyingly different arrangement.

The textured surface, created by wooden shingles, is visually varied by different patterns. A shingled band resembling a miniature mansard roof connects the veranda and bays, which might otherwise appear independent. The turned veranda posts stand out most amidst the array of spindles, gingerbread and brackets. Wooden arches over the tower windows continue the round-headed, or Renaissance, reference. Original decorative details, now lost, included cutouts under the eaves of the

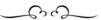

The Shand House Museum, Windsor, was constructed in 1890 by builder Joseph Taylor.

front gable and railings surrounding the second-storey verandas.

The use of wooden ornamentation like that on the Bishop's Residence is known as spindlework. A spindlework Queen Anne provides greater maintenance challenges than many other old houses, simply because there are so many more wooden elements to maintain or replace. To lose the detail of a Queen Anne is to lose the picturesque soul of the style.

The Clifford Shand House in Windsor, another spindlework Queen Anne, features robust square-section veranda posts and detailing sometimes referred to as Eastlake style. Charles Locke Eastlake, a British architect and author of the 1872 book, *Hints on Household Taste*, advocated durable, straight-line designs in architecture and furniture. The abundant exterior ornamentation of the house — it has 23 different kinds of decorative woodwork on its front façade — sets the tone for the interior. Craftsmen from the family's furniture factory created the railings and cherry wood panelling in the central stair hall.

Shand found design elements for this house in Selected Designs from Shoppell's Modern Houses, *published that same year by the Cooperative Building Plan Association in New York.*

Wooden mantelpieces in most rooms are decorative, since the house was up-to-date with central heating. It also included a new room, known as a bathroom. It too featured wood panelling, as well as modern plumbing technology: an indoor toilet, hot and cold running water, and a built-in bathtub.

Spindlework is one of three modes of exterior decoration seen on Nova Scotian Queen Annes. The second mode is referred to as Free Classic and is quite common. Generally the diagnostic feature of the Free Classic is the use of classical columns, rather than turned spindles or flat posts, to support veranda and entrance roofs. Free Classics also use a combination of decorative shingles, stick ornamentation and other decorative elements to achieve the complexity and picturesqueness required by a Queen Anne.

The Free Classic could be described as Queen Anne in exit mode, since it overlaps with other American styles of the period. The lines between them can sometimes blur, confounding the house-gazer. The 1903 design of the Women's Council House by Halifax architect James Dumaresque demonstrates the stylistic murkiness of this era. The central portico, supported by columns, suggests the Free Classic mode. At the same time, the other classical features of the house — a central door flanked by pilasters, a light over the door, a broken pediment and a Palladian window — were beginning to appear on early forms of the Colonial Revival style. The double-height columns and portico are signature elements of the developing Neoclassical Revival. And the half-timbering detail was a feature of the emerging Tudor style.

At first glance, with its square form, hipped roof, symmetrical window treatment and the central pedimented portico, the Regent Bed and Breakfast in Amherst looks Georgian Classical, like a vertically stretched version of Charles Prescott's Acacia Grove in Starr's Point. The steep pitch of the roof, paralleled by the pitch of the dormer, suggests Gothic influence. The discreet single-storey portico and columns contribute to its classical appearance. This Queen Anne Free Classic is a picturesque treatment of the classical house as conceived at the end of the nineteenth century, when trying to reproduce the original style was not the intent.

The seeming plainness of the Regent is relieved by patterned wall surfaces and gable ornament called stickwork. One sees it occasionally, either as part of a Queen Anne house or as a style unto itself. Different forms of wall coverings (shingles, clapboards) applied in varying directions are combined with

Columns rather than posts support the veranda roof of the Women's Council House in Halifax (opposite) and the Regent Bed and Breakfast in Amherst (right). This feature distinguishes the second mode of Queen Anne that occurs in Nova Scotia — the Free Classic. The three-part window over the door of the Women's Council House is a classical form known as Palladian.

Look for variations in the surface texture of any Queen Anne, whether in spindlework mode, Free Classic mode (left) or in masonry mode, such as the Charles C. Richards House in Yarmouth (above).

corner boards, brackets, trusses in gables and bands of trim under the cornice. The subtlety of the Regent's composition makes it a pleasure to examine: decorative shingles in the gable of the Regent Street bay, brackets along the cornice, a band of narrow vertical boards beneath the cornice underlined with a smooth horizontal board, a string course beneath the second-storey window and corner boards *cum* pilasters on the ground-floor bay. The Regent's array of window forms and treatments exemplifies how windows were used as ornamental elements in this period. Look elsewhere for variations of the large, square single-pane window below another window featuring a pattern of small squares or diamonds. Queen Annes often have large windows of intricate coloured and bevelled glass as a focal point above the landing in a grand staircase.

Paint is another way to achieve visual complexity with wooden Queen Annes. The preference of the period was to use darker colours

below, giving a feeling of solidity, and lighter colours above. Darker tones were used to bring out the trim and to avoid a flat effect. Projecting ornament, like bargeboard, was painted a light colour so that its contours would be contrasted against the darker shade behind.

The masonry mode of Queen Anne is the least common in Nova Scotia. Masonry Queen Annes are small in number but, true to the Queen Anne genes, they show diversity and picturesqueness in form. The gable-roofed Bread and Roses Bed and Breakfast in Annapolis Royal is Gothic in its verticality. The hipped-roof Charles C. Richards House Bed and Breakfast in Yarmouth, with its decorative wooden veranda, is a combination of masonry and spindlework. To add

Left: Coloured slates in the gable contrast not only with each other but with the brick and stone used in the Bread and Roses Bed and Breakfast in Annapolis Royal. Above: A row of Free Classic townhouses, such as this Amherst terrace, is a rare occurrence in Nova Scotia.

complexity to a masonry exterior contrasting types and colours of the brick or stone are integrated to make patterns and add texture. Sometimes there is a bas-relief in pressed terra cotta over windows or in gable ends. Other masonry Queen Annes occur in New Glasgow, Amherst and Halifax.

The size and showy nature of a Queen Anne house required a spacious lot. Most occupied suburban locations when built. A Nova Scotian exception is a row of three Queen Anne Free Classic townhouses in Amherst, abutting the Robie Street sidewalk. The row features three pediment-roofed porches, supported at the front corners by a trio of slender, turned wooden columns. Around the corner on Havelock Street is the rest of the structure, reading like a complete Queen Anne house in itself. This row was built as housing for the managers of Rhodes Curry, the largest construction company in the province at the time. Across the street, on a large lot, is a substantial Queen Anne house built by Rhodes for himself. He apparently built the housing for his employees so he could keep an eye on whether or not they were attending church regularly.

Stick, Shingle, Eclectic and Richardson-Romanesque

Although Queen Anne was the dominant style in late nineteenth-century Nova Scotia, there were other contemporary styles: Stick, Richardson-Romanesque, Shingle, Eclectic. Pure examples of these styles are relatively rare in Nova Scotia, although their design features were sometimes incorporated into Queen Anne-style houses or combined to produce distinctive hybrids. What all these styles share is an obvious pleasure in ornamented architecture, each with a different approach. It's this visual diversity that makes well-preserved, big houses of this time fun to view and provides the maintenance challenge for present-day owners.

Opposite: Shingle style houses were usually architect-designed, like this 1898 Windsor example by William Critchlow Harris. All-over shingle cladding was the common and consistent feature of the style.

Stick is a style of exterior ornamentation. It often mimics the structural elements of a medieval timber-framed building and generally features combinations of decorative boarding or shinglework or both.

The Stick style is recognized exclusively by its exterior ornamentation and does not have a distinctive house form, making the style elusive and variable. Stick was the result of a number of influences. In England it derived from half-timbered medieval architecture, emerging from the Gothic Revival around 1860. In the United States, Stick appeared by the 1870s as a cottage and railroad architectural style, influenced by pattern book imitations of Swiss chalets and the Japanese craze then sweeping the nation. This diversity of design sources gives a sense of the rampant eclecticism of the time.

Stick ornamentation often mimics, in a very approximate manner, the structural elements of a timber-framed medieval building. The "frame" elements are simply boards (sometimes with chamfered or bevelled edges) that define panels between or underneath windows or that form bands across the building and are filled in with

stickwork: boarding applied on the vertical or the diagonal, as well as on the horizontal. These panels could also be filled with clapboard or shingles, decorative or plain. The gable is often surfaced with decorative woodwork or spanned with a plain or decorated truss. Sometimes there are brackets at the eaves, often in the form of open braces. The decoration may be an ensemble of flat and turned elements, similar to that of a spindlework Queen Anne.

Of the Nova Scotian Stick houses, few are more complex than Oakdale in Maitland. At first glance the three finial-topped gables suggest a Gothic Revival house, similar to others in town. A closer look shows something different: the gables surmount a pair of dormers and a tiny centre balcony. These elements have a squareness that is Stick in sensibility. The trusses in the gable are also characteristic of the style, as is the mixture of siding techniques: vertical boarding on the top and clapboard on the bottom.

Two more examples show how varied the Stick style can be, in appearance and in quantity of

Oakdale in Maitland (opposite) and a house in Lockeport (above) illustrate the variety of approaches to Stick styling. The verticality and picturesqueness of both houses is rooted in the Gothic antecedents of this style.

ornamentation. A mixture of cladding appears on a simple but picturesque Stick house in Lockeport. Vertical board-and-batten walls contrast with decorative shingle work in the gable. The vertical boards that fill in the upper part of the recessed entrances have gaps between them, like a picket fence, and are crossed by a diagonal truss-like member.

A gable-front house in Windsor is well painted to show the horizontal and vertical bands that organize the façade, clad in a combination of clapboards and decorative shingles. There is spindlework ornamentation in the gable and the veranda. Although these houses show how the Stick style can work as a complete composition, Stick decorative elements most often appear applied to another style, as seen on the Free Classic Queen Anne Regent Bed and Breakfast in Amherst.

The Shingle style was American in origin, where it was used by architects for seaside houses in the northeastern states. The motivation for the style was the same search for beautiful,

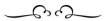

functional and appropriate forms that compelled the British Arts and Crafts Movement. In the United States it was coupled with an interest in colonial buildings. Americans had become fascinated with their pre-revolutionary architecture when they commemorated a hundred years of nationhood in 1876 with the Philadelphia Centennial Exhibition. The Shingle style was the first to draw from that built heritage. It incorporated asymmetrical forms, porches and Palladian windows from the Queen Anne; from Richardsonian-Romanesque it took arches and irregularly sculpted shapes; from the colonial heritage it borrowed and celebrated the shingle as exterior cladding. Forms and

Stick ornamentation makes this gable-front house in Windsor much more decorative than the vernacular versions that one sees across Nova Scotia. The paint scheme emphasizes the horizontal and vertical bands that organize the façade.

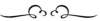

This gambrel-roofed Shingle-style house in Pugwash (above and right) is typical of the style. The tower is a mere bulge on the ground floor and only partially emerges from the roof.

compositions were varied, probably because Shingle-style houses were usually architect-designed. All-over shingle cladding is their one common and consistent element.

The Shingle style occurs occasionally in Nova Scotia. A Windsor house, designed by the architect William Critchlow Harris in 1898, is a good example with its arches, porch, irregular forms and plain shingled exterior. Harris designed a similar but smaller house on Robie Street in Halifax. Unlike the Queen Anne style, the Shingle style has little or no decorative detailing at entrances, cornices, porches or wall surfaces. The desired effect was an expansive flat surface with a picturesque silhouette.

The treatment of the tower on a gambrel-roofed Shingle-style house

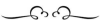

This Parrsboro house is a charming vernacular expression of the Shingle style. The asymmetry of form, the strips of three windows, the shingled porch supports and sculpted arches are Shingle features.

in Pugwash is typical of the style. The tower is a mere bulge on the ground floor and only partially emerges from the roof. The house appears to be only a single storey, since the second storey is hidden by the lower part of the roof. Imagine a shingled roof flowing into the body of the house, as it probably did when the house was built. To be faithful to the style neither the roof shingles nor the body shingles would have been painted, in order to achieve the uniformity of the surface and to emphasize the irregularity of the house shape.

The Suttles and Seawinds building in Mahone Bay demonstrates the picturesque effect of a totally shingled house. It is not in the Shingle style, although the effect of the massive house with its cross-gabled hipped roof and its variously sized gables is akin to the style. The corner boards, string courses and bracketed entrance roof are Queen Anne. When characteristics of several late Victorian styles are found in a single house, the style can be described as Eclectic. In fact, there was such a variety of decorative woodwork and form

Some late Victorian houses, like this Mahone Bay house, are stylistically difficult to pin down. In such cases the style may be described as Eclectic because characteristics of several styles are combined to create a distinctive hybrid.

used in the decades around the turn of the century that it feels sometimes that most of the houses are Eclectic. Some of this was due to indulgence in the new and plentiful millwork that resulted from improvements in woodworking technology. After 1880, mouldings and windows and doors in dozens of styles were available across Nova Scotia. Homeowners and builders were aided by many pattern books that, by "showing a great variety of design," as one 1873 book advertises, encouraged the mixing of styles. Often houses with mixed-style parentage are transitional, showing that a style shift was under way. Builders were not expecting that people a hundred years in the future would be trying to categorize and name their work.

The Richardson in the style name Richardson-Romanesque refers to the Boston architect Henry H. Richardson, who designed distinctive and expensive masonry houses in the late 1870s. The houses borrow features from early French architecture: all incorporated a round arch and most had round towers. In the 1890s, after Richardson's untimely death, a number of sympathetic architects continued working with the style in wood as well as in stone. A house built of local red sandstone in 1903 in Amherst is characteristic of Richardson's particular style.

Opposite and right: This sandstone house in Amherst is Richardson-Romanesque in style. The round arch and round tower are features borrowed from early French architecture.

Craftsman and Revival Styles

From 1900 through 1920 Nova Scotians built houses in a number of styles: Queen Anne Free Classics and Colonial Revivals tended to be large, and Four-Squares, Gable Fronts and Craftsman bungalows were on the modest side. The veranda continued to be popular, and when part of it was enclosed it became a sun porch. Wood was still the favoured building material, but more brick houses started to appear as the century progressed and the local brick producer became a housing developer to provide a market for his products. House patterns continued to be available from pattern books, mail-order businesses and magazines, and building materials were standardized. A North American continental housing market mushroomed. Pre-cut and packaged housing materials could be ordered by mail and delivered by train. All of this conspired to limit or eliminate regional building styles.

Although it was a new century, houses built in the first half of the twentieth were influenced by the same ideas and design sources familiar to the late Victorians. Many residences continued to combine classical and picturesque features. Builders combined characteristics of two or more styles in a single house. The dominant twentieth-century tastemaker in Nova Scotia was the United States rather than Britain. Most styles of this period, the Queen Anne Free Classic, Colonial Revival, Neoclassical Revival, and Dutch Colonial result from American architects and builders drawing inspiration from their colonial built heritage.

The other significant style of this period, the Craftsman, owed a great deal to the British Arts and Crafts Movement and the British Empire, but it was Americans who popularized the predominant form in this style, the Craftsman bungalow. The bungalow entered the English language and housing heritage

Nova Scotians generally followed two style trends during the first half of the 1900s, the Period Revivals (opposite) and the Craftsman (above). The house on the cover of the January 1914 issue of Bungalow *is almost identical to the Lunenburg example above.*

through the British colonial experience in India: the name and the form originally referred to a type of small, vernacular single-storey residence in Bengal, India, that had a wrap-around veranda covered by the roof. The brothers Charles and Henry Greene began designing a new form of bungalow in 1903 in California. Gustav Stickley, an American designer craftsman and supporter of the British Arts and Crafts Movement, included their designs in his magazine, *The Craftsman*. Advocates of the movement felt that good design had been lost in industrialized production and were keen to demonstrate that well-designed and well-made objects, including houses, added joy, beauty and value to everyday life.

Until the late 1920s, the bungalow was a very popular North American house type, and in Canada it was particularly favoured by British migrants to British Columbia. It is a modest house, always with a veranda that is generally full width, sometimes partially enclosed as a sun porch. It always has a gently sloping roof extending over the veranda, broad eaves and exposed rafter ends. The rafters and eaves evoke medieval English building practices, highlighting the affinity to the Arts and Crafts Movement.

Although the British Arts and Crafts Movement was the major influence on designers of the Craftsman house, another influence was oriental wooden architecture, as expressed in the veranda supports of this Halifax example.

A Lunenburg bungalow is almost identical to a house on the cover of the January 1914 issue of *Bungalow* magazine. Quite a style change from just a few years earlier when the "bump," unique to the county, held sway in Lunenburg. This gable-roofed bungalow is a common form. Two massive columns support the veranda roof, with a single line of applied beach stone that may be a whimsical reference to the classical orders. The mix of shingle, rounded beach stone (a popular decorative material for bungalows) and stucco increase the picturesque quality of this small house. The distinctive technique of alternating narrow and wide bands of shingles was commonly used on Nova Scotian Craftsman bungalows and larger Craftsman-style houses.

Columns that support bungalow veranda roofs vary in detail. Generally they are robust, of partial height, supported by piers or a low wall rising from the veranda floor. Sometimes veranda supports have sloping sides, thicker at the base than at the top. A dormer-front type bungalow in Mahone Bay, Nature's Cottage Bed and Breakfast, has veranda supports with vertical sides. The trim is flared on the ground floor windows of the front façade, giving the design a slightly Egyptian

The detailing may look decidedly Japanese, particularly in some Craftsman-style houses, because promoters of the style were also fascinated with Japanese art and building practices. The Arts and Crafts sensibility is expressed in cozy interiors with dark stained wood used for panelling and trim, built-in cupboards and fireplaces.

air. For a small house there are enough things going on to create visual interest. Builders seemed to follow pattern book plans quite accurately so excellent examples of the style occur around the province.

Watch for the vernacular form of the bungalow, particularly in the countryside. A Tatamagouche example features a shed dormer that

A Craftsman bungalow always has a gently sloping roof that extends over a full-width veranda, with broad eaves and exposed rafter ends. The columns that support the veranda roof of this Mahone Bay bungalow are but one of the numerous column variations.

runs almost the entire length of the house. Part of the veranda is enclosed to create a sun porch, a common adaptation. The eaves are not as broad as those on the high-style versions, but there are four knee-braces where the roof joins the walls in the gable ends, a style-conscious feature. A few larger Craftsman-style houses are found in Halifax and other urban centres. These robust houses express many of

The vernacular bungalow with a shed dormer occurs throughout the Nova Scotia countryside. The veranda is often partially or fully enclosed as a sun porch. The knee braces in the gable ends of this Tatamagouche example are a reference to the high-style Craftsman form.

Shingle got larger as other popular styles developed in the United States: first the Queen Anne Free Classic and then new interpretations of colonial houses. In the late nineteenth and early twentieth centuries, however, these revivals showed no intent to accurately reproduce houses from the pre-revolutionary period. Instead, both square and rectangular forms were adapted in symmetrical and asymmetrical ways with either hipped, gable or gambrel roofs, and were ornamented with adaptations of classical elements such as pedimented

the same design elements found on a bungalow, expressed in a variety of building shapes. Generally a Craftsman house is elegant and at the same time looks comfortable.

The wave of revival styles from the United States that began arriving on Nova Scotia's shores in a small way with the nineteenth-century

Pre-revolutionary American houses inspired various Colonial Revival house forms. This 1911 hipped-roof house in Lunenburg resembles Georgian Classical houses like Acacia Grove and it incorporates a wrap-around veranda.

entrances, cornices, Palladian windows, columns for veranda roof supports and updated window treatments using bay or paired windows.

The symmetrical, hipped-roof Colonial Revival form resembles Nova Scotian Georgian Classical houses like Acacia Grove. An example is the Senator Bed and Breakfast, built in 1911 in Lunenburg. The house communicates the balance and repose of a classical house with its

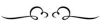

Other versions of the symmetrical hipped-roof Colonial Revival form include the Captain Angus Walters House in Lunenburg (opposite) and the very popular Four-Square form like this one in Mahone Bay (above). A Wolfville Four-Square features Craftsman details (above right).

wrap-around veranda supported by columns. Another Lunenburg example of a symmetrical, hipped-roof Colonial Revival is the house built by Angus Walters, captain of the famous schooner *Bluenose.* The understated yet elegant veranda columns are a good example of how columns that support entry porches and verandas are treated in this style. The house sits right next to the sidewalk, like the original colonial houses in Lunenburg built about 150 years earlier. In contrast,

just a few blocks away, the Senator is sited more characteristically in the middle of a large suburban lot in Lunenburg's "new town."

A plainer and generally smaller version of the symmetrical hipped-roof house is commonly known as a Four-Square. This type was popular both as an urban and a farm-house style for about 30 years, starting in the late 1890s. It has some presence but is modest compared to a Queen Anne. "Four-Square" accurately describes its solid, boxy, two-storey form. Often it has a central dormer and a full-width veranda, with unpretentious columns or posts. The veranda is usually the only element that provides visual interest and varies with the amount and type of detail. When there is no veranda the style looks quite austere. The Heart's Desire Bed and Breakfast in Mahone Bay is but one of hundreds of Four-Squares in Nova Scotia. A Wolfville Four-Square demonstrates how the form can also be associated with another style: in this case, the exposed rafter ends under both roofs, an exterior chimney clad in stone and the charcoal-grey paint colour are features borrowed from the Craftsman style.

A charming one-storey house style seen in Nova Scotia is characterized by a colonnaded veranda, a hipped roof and either one prominent central dormer or, as in the case of an example in

The symmetrical hipped-roof form also occurs as a one-storey cottage, like this Bridgewater example (above), as well as being the basis for this Eclectic house in Truro (right) that mixes characteristics of the Queen Anne Free Classic, Shingle and Craftsman styles.

Bridgewater, one dormer per side. Sometimes this form occurs with part of the veranda enclosed as a sun porch. The form may be called either a one-storey, hipped-roof Colonial Revival or a one-storey Four-Square. The lovely oriel-bay window on the Bridgewater house is borrowed from the Tudor vocabulary. The ground-floor windows on the front façade are a common early twentieth-century form, with a large pane below and patterned panel above.

An ambiguous 1919 house in Truro exemplifies the mixture of styles from this period that can confound the house-gazer. With its picturesque composition, it looks at first like a Queen Anne Free Classic. Recognizable classical elements include a squarish shape, hipped roof, Palladian window and columns supporting the veranda roof. Yet the dormer treatment, with its curved walls and recessed window, is a feature of the Shingle style. The roof pitch and exposed rafters are features of the Craftsman. There were a lot of squarish, hipped-roofed

Following published studies of original Colonial houses in the 1920s and 1930s, Revivals more closely resembled their colonial antecedents, like this two-storey house in Windsor (left) and the Halifax example (right).

houses built in the first half of the twentieth century. The fact that they can range from upper-class estates on the Northwest Arm in Halifax to workers' houses in Sydney Mines demonstrates the flexibility of the form.

During the period from 1910 through the 1930s, designers began to pay attention to the specific shape and ornamentation of colonial houses, following published studies of American colonial buildings. Colonial Revival houses of this period more closely resembled the originals and set the style for hundreds if not thousands of white, shingled and clapboarded houses in suburban North America. One- and two-storey houses, like the Fiddlehead Bed and Breakfast in Windsor and the offices for St. Mary's Continuing Education in Halifax, look similar to Classical Vernacular types from the end of the eighteenth century.

The interest in authenticity emerged in Nova Scotia as well in the 1920s and 1930s. The beginning of a preservation sensibility in the province can be traced to this period, with the work of people like Arthur W. Wallace and Mary Allison Prescott. Wallace was a McGill-trained architect who began in 1924 to make measured drawings of a number of early buildings, including Mount Uniacke, Government House and Acacia Grove. Mary Allison Prescott bought Acacia Grove, her great grandfather's then-derelict house in Starr's Point, and Wallace was involved architecturally with the renovations of this house in the mid-1930s.

In 1938, local historian and author Elizabeth Coward and her banker husband Sam built a well-detailed one and one-half-storey Colonial Revival in her native Bridgetown. A garage was connected to one end of the house by a breezeway and a small, roofed sun-deck extended from the other end giving it the desired silhouette of a vernacular house that had been added to over the years. The house was modern in its layout but fitted comfortably with houses in the town

This Colonial Revival was built by Bridgetown historian Elizabeth Coward and her husband in 1938.

The steep pitch of the roof and absence of eaves on this Colonial Revival house, designed in 1930 by Halifax architect Andrew Cobb, give the house an authentic effect.

that were over a hundred years its senior. Both Coward and Prescott enhanced their homes with well designed flower gardens. They would have been influenced by publications like the American magazine *House & Garden*, which in the late 1930s was dedicating whole issues to the historical sources of Colonial architecture and decoration, including ads for Colonial furnishings and prefabricated houses with "many designs in the pleasing New England tradition."

Andrew Cobb, a popular Halifax architect, designed many houses between 1909 and his death in 1943 corresponding to the popular styles of the day: Craftsman, Tudor and a series of Colonial Revivals. The steep pitch of the roof and lack of eaves on a Colonial Revival house he designed in 1930 give the house an authentic effect and a timeless quality. Cobb's classical entrance with the elongated broken pediment is sprightly and updated. Cobb houses are usually well-detailed inside, with lots of built-in cupboards and features.

The concern for authenticity in Colonial Revivals that was present in the 1920s and 1930s faded in the 1940s and 1950s. The Colonial Revival style during this period is exemplified by a Halifax house called a Second-storey Overhang. It doesn't look much like the hand-hewn timber-framed medieval version built by early colonists in seventeenth-century New England, and known in England as a jettied front. The first storey is faced with masonry, the second with wood. The ell is a common Revival feature, functioning as sunroom or den: the broad stone chimney on the gable end suggests a den in this instance. Garages and other consequences of the car had become a common feature.

A medieval, timber-framed jettied-front house was the antecedent for this Revival house type now known as a Second-storey Overhang.

Nova Scotians also built many houses in the Dutch Colonial Revival style. New York had once been a Dutch colony, and remembering this the Americans revived the Dutch Colonial tradition. In this case authenticity was never an issue. Rather, what characterized this style was the gambrel roof form, used in late seventeenth- and early eighteenth-century England as well as on the European continent. It had appeared earlier as a central feature of the Shingle style, where the roof worked both as a picturesque element and a colonial reference.

The gambrel roof is a gable roof with two slopes, allowing more room on the second floor than a plain gable roof does, particularly when it is combined with a wide shed dormer. This may explain why the Dutch Colonial style was so popular across Nova Scotia, appearing most often in a side-gable form. A steeply pitched gambrel roof, like that on a generously sized Halifax example, contains a full second storey of floor space. The continuous shed dormer with its many windows emerges neatly from the upper slope of the roof. The entrance with sidelights and fanlight would be comfortable on a Georgian Classical home. There is usually no difficulty in telling these twentieth-century gambrel-roofed houses from the few eighteenth-century survivals in such places as Lunenburg, Liverpool, Annapolis Royal and Grand Pré. The same is not always true of some small Revival Cape Cods that, when well sited and authentically detailed, do look like the real thing.

The Tudor Revival houses built by Nova Scotians during the first decades of the twentieth century varied in size, form and ornamentation, but generally all are intended to appeal to the eye.

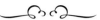

A one-storey house in Tusket is a modern interpretation of the Classical Vernacular. It mimics a house that's been added to over time, like Simeon Perkins' house in Liverpool. At the same time, it has the casual convenience of a 1950s ranch house.

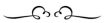

This gambrel-roofed Revival style, known as Dutch Colonial, appears in small, medium and large sizes all over Nova Scotia.

This 1918 Tudor Revival house was designed by architect Andrew Cobb. The style is derived from half-timbered English cottages and houses of the late 1600s and early 1700s.

Tudor is a revival style that mimics cottages and houses primarily from the late seventeenth and early eighteenth centuries, known as the Jacobean period, when timber framing was structural rather than decorative. Just as Acadian cottages in Bellisle were timber framed with walls filled in with a mixture of clay and hay, so the English structures were framed and filled with various materials. The thickness of the

Each of the various house forms in the ten-block Hydrostone District in Halifax have an English-cottage feel because of steep pitched gable roofs, some half-timbering and a mix of stucco and other exterior finishes. The district is designed in the garden-suburb style introduced by Richard Norman Shaw, the same architect who designed the very first Queen Anne–style house.

hand-hewn timbers determined the thickness of the walls. Two hundred and fifty years on, the thin balloon framing system that replaced timber framing was hidden between the interior finish and an exterior of stucco, wood, brick or a combination of any or all of these materials. The "timber framing" then became an exterior decorative element. The pattern of the half timbering is often abstract, or merely a gesture. Rarely does it accurately reflect the structure of a true half-timbered building. Half-timbering decoration is a giveaway feature for Tudor Revival houses when it appears, but it does not occur on all examples.

Some Tudor Revival houses have steep gable roofs, echoing medieval times. In a few instances the gable roofs are hipped, suggesting the silhouette of a thatched-roof cottage. Entrances in the Tudor style are usually accentuated in some way, often with a porch with a steeply pitched roof and an arched, recessed door. Decorative wooden doors are usually pierced by a small window, glazed with several smaller panes of glass. Some Tudor Revival houses, like an example in Truro, evoke English "cottageness" rather than a particular historical example. The front façade is dominated by pointed gables and the half timbering is minimal. This house is stuccoed, but it has a double in Halifax that is clad in wood. Wooden Tudor houses are often painted in distinctive colours.

A two-storey side-gabled house designed in 1918 by Andrew Cobb is an example of his work in the Tudor Revival style. It features stylized half timbering on one gable and in a band across the front façade. The stucco surface below the half timbering is very heavily textured. The picturesque entrance porch is flanked by slightly bowed windows in recessed rectangular window openings. This house has a number of Tudor kin on neighbouring Halifax streets, but each is different in form, scale and decoration. An exact copy of the Cobb design can be found across the harbour in Dartmouth. Tudor remains one of the most popular and marketable styles in North America, adaptable to starter

Tudor Revival houses usually have steep gable roofs and an arched, recessed entrance. There may also be some decorative half timbering, although often abstract and minimal, as in this Truro cottage (right and opposite).

houses or palatial and rambling "stockbroker Tudors" with multi-car garages.

A whole district with Tudor-style buildings in Halifax is the area known as the Hydrostone. It was designed in the garden-suburb style, first used by Richard Norman Shaw in England in 1875. The layout of the ten-block Hydrostone district is consistent with Shaw's ideal: modest houses on streets with trees and public green space in front, narrow service lanes behind. There are 324 houses in the district and the pleasing variation in forms and details demonstrate that it is possible to design a relatively high-density housing development that is not tedious in its repetition. That it has remained a desirable place to live for 80 years is also a testament to the concept.

The houses include single-family dwellings interspersed with semi-detached, two-family and terrace houses featuring a variety of dormers, windows and trim. They have an English-cottage feel, with some half timbering and a mix of exterior surface finishes. The plan was the response of Montreal architect Gordon Ross to the need for replacement housing following the devastation of north end Halifax by the December 1917 explosion. The name "Hydrostone" comes from the major building material used in the project, a hollow concrete block manufactured across the harbour in Eastern Passage.

The Great Depression of the 1930s ensured that few new houses were constructed, particularly in avant-garde styles. It's rare in Nova Scotia to see a twentieth-century Art Moderne house with its characteristic flat roof, rounded corners and wrap-around windows; rarer still to see one in original 1930s condition. A few altered survivors are just recognizable. When the Second World War arrived it brought the need for lots of new houses, quickly. The solution was provided by small prefabricated houses resembling one-storey Classical Vernaculars. Many of these houses are still in use in communities that were particularly busy during the war effort, such as Yarmouth, Halifax and Trenton.

In the 1950s, major changes occurred. The need to provide housing for an increasing number of young families filled suburbs across Nova Scotia and the continent with new Modern and Ranch styles and familiar Period Revival styles. We tend not to regard these thirty- to fifty-year-old houses as part of the housing heritage, but the fact is that styles have changed yet again and many of these houses are being renovated. It's time for house-gazers to start looking at this group of houses, now settled among mature trees and often over-mature shrubs. There are lots of discoveries to be made, particularly the houses designed by local architects.

Further Reading

Mary Byers and Margaret McBurney. *Atlantic Hearth: Early Homes and Families of Nova Scotia.* Toronto: University of Toronto Press, 1994.

Margaret R. Conrad and James K. Hillier. *Atlantic Canada: A Region in the Making.* Toronto: Oxford University Press, 2001.

Brenda Dunn. "Acadia Architecture in Port Royal" in *Heritage*, Summer 2002. Volume V Number 3.

Peter Ennals and Deryck Holdsworth. *Homeplace: The Making of the Canadian Dwelling over Three Centuries.* Toronto: University of Toronto Press, 1998.

Judith Fingard, Janet Guildford and David Sutherland. *Halifax: the First 250 Years.* Halifax: Formac Publishing, 1999.

Alan Gowans. *The Comfortable House: North American Suburban Architecture, 1890–1930.* Cambridge, Mass.: MIT Press, 1986.

Pat Lotz, ed. *Affairs with Old Houses.* Halifax: Heritage Trust of Nova Scotia and Nimbus Publishing, 1999.

Terry James and Bill Plaskett. *Buildings of Old Lunenburg.* Halifax: Nimbus Publishing, 1996.

Harold Kalman. *A Concise History of Canadian Architecture.* Toronto: Oxford University Press, 2000.

Joann Latremouille. *Pride of Home: The Working Class Housing Tradition in Nova Scotia 1749–1949.* Photographs by Kathleen Flanagan. Illustrations by Joan Rentoul. Hantsport: Lancelot Press, 1986.

Mary K. MacLeod and James O. St. Clair. *No Place Like Home: The Life and Times of Cape Breton Heritage Houses.* Sydney: University College of Cape Breton Press, 1992.

———. *Pride of Place: The Life and Times of Cape Breton Heritage Houses.* Sydney: University College of Cape Breton Press, 1994.

Virginia and Lee McAlester. *A Field Guide to American Houses.* New York: Alfred Knopf, 1986.

Elizabeth Pacey. *Georgian Halifax.* Hantsport: Lancelot Press, 1987.

Elizabeth Pacey and Alvin Comiter. *Historic Halifax.* Willowdale: Anthony R Hawke, 1988.

———. *Landmarks: Historic Buildings of Nova Scotia.* Halifax: Nimbus Publishing, 1994.

Allen Penney. *Houses of Nova Scotia: An Illustrated Guide to Architectural Style Recognition.* Halifax: Formac Publishing and the Nova Scotia Museum, 1989.

———. *The Simeon Perkins House: An Architectural Interpretation 1767–1987.* Curatorial Report Number 60. Halifax: Nova Scotia Museum, 1987.

———. "Towards an Architectural Interpretation of the Uniacke Homesite" in *Uniacke Estate Seminar, 1989.* Curatorial Report Number 70. Halifax: Nova Scotia Museum, 1989.

Barbara R. Robertson. *Gingerbread and House Finish of Every Description.* Halifax: Nova Scotia Museum, 1990.

———. *Sawpower: Making Lumber in the Sawmills of Nova Scotia.* Halifax: Nimbus Publishing and the Nova Scotia Museum, 1986.

Arthur W. Wallace. *An Album of Drawings of Early Buildings in Nova Scotia.* Halifax: Heritage Trust of Nova Scotia and the Nova Scotia Museum, 1976.

Jean Weir. *Rich in Interest and Charm: The Architecture of Andrew Randall Cobb 1876–1943.* Halifax: Art Gallery of Nova Scotia, 1990.

Index

Acacia Grove, Starr's Point 21, 95, 113, 117
Acadia University 45
Acadians 10-11, 34, 36, 123
Adam, Robert 45
American Revolution 17, 45
Amherst 11, 13, 37, 43, 87, 89, 95, 97, 101, 107
Anglican church architecture 53-54
Annapolis Royal 11, 23, 61, 68-69, 96-97, 120
Annapolis Valley 39
Art Moderne style 126
Arts and Crafts Movement 101-02, 109-10

Barrington 10, 47, 49
Bay of Fundy 43, 49
Belleisle 11, 123
Bishop's Residence, Yarmouth 90-92
Bracketed style 64, 67
Bridgetown 117-18
Bridgewater 116
Brown, J.L. 45

Cap Le Moine 36
Cape Breton 10, 34, 36-37
"Cape Cod" houses 26, 29, 83, 120
Cape Sable 10
The Cedars, Hantsport 59-60
Cheticamp 36
Churchill House see The Cedars
Clare 34
classical orders, described 17
Classical Vernacular houses see Vernacular styles
Cobb, Andrew 119-20, 123, 125
Coffinscroft 47
Colchester County 9
Cole Harbour Heritage Farm Museum 26
Colonial Revival styles 14, 29, 34, 95, 109, 112-13, 115-116
Comeauville 89
company houses see workers' houses
Connecticut 28
construction techniques
    balloon framing 10, 87, 125
    bousillage (clay-rich mud and salt marsh hay) 11
    charpente (half-timbered framing) 11
    coulisse 10, 26, 28
    pièce-sur-pièce (horizontal log fill) 11
    piquet (vertical log construction) 11
    post-and-beam 10
    prefabricated 27, 37, 126
    timber framing 10, 99, 123

Cossit House Museum, Sydney 23
cottages 12
Craftsman style 11, 14, 109-12, 116-18, 120
Cumberland County 9-10, 11

Dartmouth 125
Dickie House, Maitland 55-56
Downing, Andrew Jackson 12, 55, 59, 63
    Cottage Residences (1842) 12
    The Architecture of Country Houses (1850) 12
Dumaresque, James 95
Dutch Colonial Revival style 109, 120, 122

Eastlake, Charles Locke Hints on Household Taste 92
Eclectic style 99, 102, 104-107, 116

Farish, James 11, 28
    Yarmouth, 1821 11
Federal style see Georgian Classical style
Four-Square style 109, 115-117
furniture 85

garden-suburb style 126
Georgian Classical style 12, 17-23, 30, 35, 39-40, 45, 51-52, 64, 70, 73-74, 95, 113, 120
German settlement 9
Girvan Bank, Annapolis Royal 23, 52
Glace Bay Miners Museum 36
Gothic Revival style 12, 25, 41, 49, 51-57, 59, 62, 83-84, 101
Government House, Halifax 17, 19-20, 23, 29, 117
Gowrie House, Sydney Mines 14
Grand Étang 36
Grand Pré 15, 27-30, 120
"Greek Gothics" (hybrid style) 49
Greek Revival style 11-12, 35, 43-49, 64-65, 77, 84
Greenwood Cottage, Sherbrooke 12, 54

Halifax 13, 17, 19-20, 27, 37, 40, 48, 59, 62-64, 69-70, 73-79, 95, 97, 110-11, 117, 119-20, 124-26
Hammond, William 47
Harris, William Critchlow 99, 103
heating 8, 11-12, 28, 75
Heritage Conservation Districts 15
Heritage Property Act 15
Heritage Trust of Nova Scotia 5
Hillsdale, Annapolis Royal 61-62
Historic Restoration Society, Annapolis Royal 11
Hydrostone District, Halifax 124, 126

Inverness 37
Iona 34

Italianate style 12, 41, 49, 59-65, 67, 73, 77-78, 83-84, 89

Kentville 11
Kluskap 9

Lake Ainslie 57
Liverpool 9, 25, 27, 47, 120-21
Lockeport 45-47, 101
Londonderry 13
Loyalists 9, 23, 30, 45
Lunenburg 10, 15, 22-23, 26, 30, 81-85, 110, 113, 115, 120
    Bump houses 81-85, 110
Lunenburg County 28, 84-85

MacDonald House, Lake Ainslie 57
Mahone Bay 102, 104, 110-11, 115-16
Maitland 12, 15, 43, 45, 47-48, 54-55, 59, 64, 67, 69, 101
Margaree Forks 56
Mount Uniacke 17, 19-21, 117
Murray Manor, Yarmouth 52
museums (listed) 15

Neoclassical Revival style 95, 109
New England 9, 25-26, 49, 85, 87, 120
New Glasgow 11, 13, 40, 97
New Ross 12, 28
north-end railway station, Halifax 69
Nova Scotia Museum 5, 17

paint schemes 33-34, 49, 96
Palladian style see Georgian Classical style
Parrsboro 43, 104
pattern books 12-13, 25, 46-47, 85, 93, 107, 109
Period Revivals see Colonial Revival styles
Perkins, Simeon 9, 25, 27-28
Pictou 37, 39-41, 54, 70
Port Hastings 34
Port Hood 40-41
Port La Tour 47
Prescott House see Acacia Grove
Prescott, Charles Ramage 10, 21, 95
Prescott, Mary Allison 117, 120
Princes Lodge 51
Pryor Terrace row houses, Halifax 73-76
Pugwash 103

Queen Anne style 11-12, 25, 87-97, 99, 103-04, 124
    Free Classic mode 93, 95-97, 101, 109, 112, 116
    masonry mode 96-97
    spindlework mode 91-93, 97, 101

Ranch style 121, 126
Regency style see Georgian Classical style
Richardson, Henry H. 107
Richardson-Romanesque style 99, 102
Rochefort settlement 9
Rosebank Cottage, New Ross 12, 28, 34
Ross-Thomson House, Shelburne 30, 32

Saint George's Round Church, Halifax 51
Saint Malo settlement 9
"saltbox" houses 25, 27
Scots settlement 9-10, 40
Scottish House style 39-41
Second Empire style 12, 67-71, 77-78, 83-84
Second World War 37, 126
Shand House 92-93
Shaw, Richard Norman 87, 124, 126
Shelburne 30
Sherbrooke 12, 52-54
Shingle style 99, 101-104, 107, 116, 120
shipbuilding 49, 59, 64, 85
Simeon Perkins House, Liverpool 25, 27, 121
Starr's Point 21, 95, 113, 117
Stellarton 37
Stewart House, Grand Pré 29-30, 32
Stick style 99, 101
Sydney 13, 23
Sydney Mines 117

Tatamagouche 110
Trenton 37, 126
Truro 11, 15, 69, 89, 116, 125
Tudor Revival style 95, 120-21, 123, 125-26
Tusket 121

Uniacke Estate Museum Park 17

Vernacular styles 10-11, 25-37, 83, 117, 121, 126

Wallace 34-35
Wentworth, Governor John 10
window styles, described 32
Windsor 92, 99, 101-03, 117
Wolfville 45
Women's Council House, Halifax 95
woodworking technology 12, 56, 78, 87, 91
workers' houses 37, 117

Yarmouth 11, 15, 28, 34, 37, 52, 60, 90, 96-97, 126
Yorkshire settlement 9

Zwicker House, Lunenburg 83-85